MAKING **BREAD** TOGETHER

MAKING **BREAD** TOGETHER

Step-by-step recipes for fun and simple breads to make with children

EMMANUEL HADJIANDREOU **photography by Steve Painter**

RYLAND PETERS & SMALL
LONDON • NEW YORK

DEDICATION

To my amazing wife Lisa and my wonderful 8-year-old boy Noah.
You both bring a lot of laughter and joy to my world.

Design, Photography and Prop Styling
Steve Painter
Commissioning Editor Nathan Joyce
Production Gary Hayes
Art Director Leslie Harrington
Editorial Director Julia Charles

US Recipe Testers Susan Stuck and Cathy Seward
Indexer Hilary Bird

First published in 2014
by Ryland Peters & Small
20–21 Jockey's Fields
London WC1R 4BW
and
519 Broadway, 5th Floor
New York, NY 10012

www.rylandpeters.com

10 9 8 7 6 5 4 3 2 1

Text © Emmanuel Hadjiandreou
Design and photographs
© Ryland Peters & Small 2014

ISBN 978 1 84975 485 9

A catalogue record for this book is available from the
British Library.
A cataloging-in-progress record is available from the
Library of Congress.

Printed and bound in China

Notes
• All spoon measurements are level, unless otherwise
specified.
• Ovens should be preheated to the specified
temperature. Recipes in this book were tested using a
fan/convection oven. If using a regular oven, follow the
manufacturer's instructions for adjusting temperatures.
• All eggs are UK medium, US large unless otherwise
specified. Recipes containing raw or partially cooked egg
should not be served to the very young, very old, anyone
with a compromised immune system or pregnant women.

contents

Introduction

My first book – ***How to Make Bread*** – was a collection of 26 years of my baking career. I travelled and worked in many different baking environments before settling in the UK, learning a great many new techniques and recipes which has allowed me to experiment and create the loaves in both my first book and this book. In this new book I am in some ways going back to the basics – trying to show people young and old, how to make bread. As a teacher you have to think of all your pupils and the many questions they might ask. I hope this book will help provide answers to many of those questions.

I realized through the enormous response and positive feedback for ***How to Make Bread*** that I had opened the doors to baking for many people who never believed they could bake, and made them feel confident in making their own bread. I love hearing from people who are working through my first book and receiving e-mails with photos of the breads they've made. They tell me of their satisfaction when they take the loaf out of the oven, tapping it on the bottom to check for the hollow sound, and the delicious freshly baked bread smell that takes over the room. One woman wrote to me enclosing pictures of the different bread she had made each weekend while she worked through the whole book. After she got through all the recipes, she sent me an e-mail asking for my permission to change a recipe and add a new ingredient to change the flavour. I was thrilled she had made all the breads in my book and that I had given her the foundations to experiment and I encouraged her to carry on. This made me extremely proud. She had definitely caught the baking bug.

One of the greatest delights I experience is teaching people to make "real" bread for the first time, the sheer joy on their faces when they take their first loaf out of the oven. The bread might be a little rustic-looking or misshapen, but that's ok because you made it and you know exactly what went into it from the beginning. I say "real" bread because a lot of the bread today has lost the respect it once had. The supermarket bread is mass-produced and churned out with many more ingredients, additives and preservatives in it than the fresh, simple and tasty recipes you'll learn how to make in this book.

I hope that you'll enjoy this book, not only for the tasty recipes, but also for the fun you'll have making the different types of bread! This book is designed for parents and children to make the recipes together. Older children can follow the instructions themselves and ask an adult for help in the places that we've specified. It's a good idea to start with the Basic Bread recipe as you'll use many of the techniques you learn here later on.

Baking is a craft that everybody can pick up, but if you have the enthusiasm and willingness to learn, you'll know it for the rest of your life. Remember that time, patience and great ingredients are vital components of great bread!

Have fun and happy baking!

getting started

Tools and Equipment

Accuracy is really important in bread baking. For this reason, I have given all ingredients in metric weights first (including salt, yeast and liquids), followed by American cups and/or ounces, teaspoons or tablespoons.

Precision electronic scales: If you choose to weigh your bread-making ingredients (rather than measure them in cups and spoons), **which I highly recommend**, you want scales that can weigh between 1 g and about 3 kg. They tend to come in 1-g, 2-g and 5-g graduation, so make sure you buy scales with a 1-g graduation for the most accurate measurement of ingredients like yeast, salt and water. When weighing out your ingredients, make sure they are gram perfect to eliminate any mistakes also, make sure you weigh the heavier ingredients first with the lighter ones on top.

Bowls: Plastic, metal and glass bowls are all fine to use. Make sure you have one large mixing bowl (approximately 2-litre/8-cup capacity) and at least two small mixing bowls (approximately 1-litre/4-cup capacity). You want to be able to fit one bowl on top of the other snugly. You can either turn the smaller one upside-down and put it inside the bigger bowl, or you can turn the larger one upside down and place it over the smaller one. I find this the most convenient way to mix wet and dry ingredients, as well as providing an easy covering while the dough rises. When using metal and glass bowls, rinse them out to warm them up with hot water if they have been stored in a cold cupboard.

Loaf pans: 500 g/6 x 4-in. (or 1-lb) and 1 kg/8½ x 4½-in. (or 2-lbs.) capacities are what we mainly use in this book.

These are my tips when working with loaf pans: Firstly, always grease your pans even if they are non-stick as it is really frustrating if your loaf sticks when trying to take it out of the pan. Another tip: don't wash them with soapy water if they are dirty, just rinse them with hot water and let them dry out in a hot oven. And one more tip, the darker your pans are, the better they will absorb the heat compared with a new, shiny one. To work out how much dough will fit into a loaf pan, add up all your ingredients including the water i.e. 500 g of mixture will fit a 500 g/1 lb. pan. The dough should fill the pan about ¾ of the way up. I highly recommend using the right size pan for your mixture, because if you're making a small loaf in a big pan, it will turn out flat.

Roasting pan: You will need to put a cup of water in this to create steam in your oven. Put the pan on the bottom of your oven before preheating it.

Shower cap: A disposable shower cap is a very useful tool! Use it for covering the mixing bowl while the dough rises and the loaf pan when the loaf rises before baking in the oven. It can also be re-used many times. Clingfilm/plastic wrap can also be used as an alternative.

Plastic dough scraper: A dough scraper is one of the most important pieces of equipment you need for bread making. This is used for scraping out all the dough and stray ingredients cleanly from the edge of the mixing bowl. It can even be used for shaping and kneading.

Metal dough scraper (Scotch scraper) or sharp serrated knife: A metal dough scraper makes dividing dough accurate and easy, but a sharp serrated knife works well, too.

Danish whisk: With its stiff stainless steel wire head, this is an excellent tool for mixing both the dry and wet ingredients, helping to break up any lumps in the process.

Proofing/dough-rising baskets: These come in various shapes and sizes and are used to hold the dough during proofing (the final dough-rise step before baking). They also create attractive patterns on the crust. Proofing/dough-rising baskets are made from a variety of different materials. These baskets are not essential to bread making but are a good investment for an enthusiastic baker. Always remember to flour your basket before placing the dough into it to stop the dough from sticking.

Bread or Pizza Peel: Use this to slide the bread into and out of a hot oven.

As well as the more specialist pieces of equipment above, you will also need many of these common kitchen items.

Baking trays/sheets
Balloon whisk
Chopping/cutting board
Clingfilm/plastic wrap

Deep muffin trays/pans
Fine sieve/strainer or flour sifter
Kitchen timer
Large knife
Measuring jug/pitcher or cups
Measuring spoons
Palette knife
Muffin cases
Non-stick parchment or silicon paper

Pastry brush
Rolling pin
Round cake pan (16 cm/7 in. diameter)
Saucepans
Scissors
Wire rack for cooling
Wooden spoon

Flour Power

Just as a builder needs concrete to make part of a house, so a baker needs flour to make bread. And both concrete and flour need water to make them work properly. Once you add water, the magic begins! On page 67, you can discover the different parts of wheat and how it grows. Once the grain has been stripped from the grass, it is left to dry out and then it is sent to a miller, who is responsible for grinding grain into a powder – that's what flour is! The miller takes a sample of the wheat and grinds it to check that it is good enough – it needs to have lots of protein in it to make good bread. Then he cleans the grain to remove straw, animal droppings, metal and seeds.

Finally, the outer "husk" or shell is removed, leaving a nice clean berry to be milled into flour. Now he checks how dry the berry is: if it is too dry, he will put some moisture into it to make it easier to grind.

There are 2 ways to make flour. One is "stone grinding" and the other is "roller" milling.

Stone-ground means that the grain is squashed between 2 stones that are powered by wind, water and sometimes by hand. It is up to the miller to decide if the flour will be coarse (a bit rough) or fine (smooth); if he sets the stones very close together, he will get a finer flour, but if he sets the stones further apart, the flour will be coarser. Stone-ground white flour is made when you pass fine wholemeal/whole-wheat flour through fine sieves.

A

B

C

A grain

B using a mini stone mill

C stone-ground flour

D wheat berries

E coarsely chopped wheat

F coarse semolina

G stone-ground wholemeal/whole-wheat flour

H stone-ground white flour

It will never be completely white because there will always be tiny amounts of bran (the hard outer layer or skin of the wheat berry) in the flour. Stone-ground flour is healthier for you as it retains all the natural vitamins and oils in the grain. This is because everything that goes in one side gets ground up and comes out the other side, and nothing is lost or thrown away. Most white flour is **roller milled**. The grain is crushed through a series of metal rollers and sieves. The first time, it is crushed with rollers with deep grooves cut into them so that the bran and germ (reproductive part that forms a seed) are removed and then sifted out. Then the grooves of the metal rollers get finer as well as the sieves. The grain is split up into different parts: bran, wheat germ, coarse semolina, fine semolina and finally white flour. To make wholemeal (whole-wheat) flour, all the parts of the grain are put back together again.

The Other Stars of the Show

Flour isn't the only star of the show! Water, yeast and salt are also crucial ingredients when it comes to making bread. Water brings all the ingredients together, while salt adds flavour and texture, but it's the yeast that provides the real magic, transforming a raw lump of dough into a lovely loaf of bread!

Water: the foundation of breadmaking

Water dissolves and changes other ingredients so they can work and transform into other things. It brings all the ingredients together and activates the yeast used to make the bread rise. When water is combined with the dry flour mixture, the proteins gluten and gliadin start to form, which is what makes dough elastic and easy to shape. The water also brings out the starch (white milky liquid), which is the food source for the yeast. You need to be careful with the temperature of the water you use when it comes to yeast. Really cold water will slow the yeast down, while heat will kill it. A hand-warm temperature (between 30°C/86°F–37°C/99°F) is perfect. If the water is too cold, mix it with a little boiled water to get it to a hand-warm temperature (**ask an adult to help with this**).

Make sure you can drink the water you use to make your bread. If you can't drink it, the yeast will not like it. If you can't drink it, use bottled water.

Always remember, you can add water to a recipe, but you can't take it out. It's better to do this rather than adding extra flour in the beginning as this will change the recipe. So as a rule, I always dissolve or activate the yeast in about ¾ of the water asked for in the recipe, then I add the flour mixture and mix slowly. If all the flour has been incorporated and it's a bit dry, add a little more water from the ¼ water you have reserved. If you find that you have used all the water and the mixture is still too dry, you can add some more water but remember to keep a record of how much you have added for next time.

Yeast: the magic ingredient

If water is the foundation, and flour the concrete, then yeast must be the builder. Yeast is a fungus – a living micro-organism made of tiny cells (that you can only see under a microscope). These cells have the ability to divide and form more and more cells extremely quickly. When yeast is added to flour, it converts the starch in the flour into simple sugars, feeding the tiny yeast cells, which then multiply rapidly. A by-product of this feeding process is the release of carbon dioxide and alcohol. This is known as 'fermentation', and it's this amazing process that makes the dough rise.

There are a number of different types of yeast available: liquid yeast; fresh yeast; crumbly yeast; dried/active dry yeast; quick dry yeast; and frozen dry yeast. The yeasts home bakers use are: fresh yeast; dried/active dry yeast; and quick dry yeast.

Fresh yeast, which is also known as compressed yeast, comes in a block. It has a putty consistency and is beige in colour. Organic fresh yeast will be darker in colour. Fresh yeast can be obtained from your local baker, supermarket or health food shop. It's really important to keep it refrigerated in a sealed container, because otherwise it may affect the other items in your fridge. It's also a good idea to write the date on the packet of yeast so you know how long you've had it. If the yeast is left open when you are working with it, dark patches may appear on the surface. If they do, just cut off the dark patches before use. Likewise, if small bits of mould appear on the block of yeast, remove the mould before use. When the yeast goes very mouldy, it's past its best so throw it away!

Dried/active dry yeast normally comes in granular form in a small tin or package. This yeast has to be soaked in warm water to activate it. When you are making bread and using this type of yeast, put the amount required in the recipe into the warm water, and allow it to soak. Don't stir or try and dissolve the yeast, just leave it to soak in the warm water. After around 10 minutes, it will float to the top and small bubbles will appear on the surface. Make sure it is completely dissolved before adding the dry ingredients.

Instant/quick dry yeast and **fast-acting yeast** come vacuum-packed or in sachets, either in powder form or as small balls. They are designed to go straight into the flour and do not need to be dissolved or activated. Fast-acting yeast contains vitamin C and other preservatives, which makes it work faster. I prefer instant/quick dry yeast as it is just pure dried yeast with an anti-caking agent to stop it getting lumpy when it's added to liquid. Make sure you add either of these types of yeast to the flour and not on top of the salt, as the salt might kill it. Keep these types of yeast in a sealed container and store in the refrigerator, like the fresh yeast. **If you want to use either instant/quick dry yeast or fast-acting yeast in the recipes in this book, use the same quantity as stated for dried/active dry yeast.**

Salt: the all-rounder

Salt adds flavour, works as a preservative and helps give the crust colour when the loaf is baking. Salt also reacts with the gluten in the dough making it stronger and more elastic. Bread made with no salt tends to have a dull colour and goes stale much quicker. When using fresh yeast, remember never to mix it directly with salt, as the salt will actually start cooking the yeast! Also when dissolving the yeast in the liquid mixture never add the salt to it, but rather mix the salt into the flour mixture.

The Magic Balloon

This experiment will both show and tell you about the amazing process going on in a lifeless looking bottle with a small piece of dough inside. All you need is a regular balloon, a transparent glass or plastic bottle and a small piece of freshly made raw bread dough.

Ingredients:

50 g/1¾ oz. raw dough from the Basic Bread recipe (page 22)

Equipment:

1 small bottle, for example a milk bottle or plastic bottle (you won't need the cap or lid), with an opening 2 cm/¾ in. wide

1 balloon

You can use any freshly made raw bread dough (dough containing yeast rather than sourdough works better, though), so it's easiest to do the experiment when you're planning to make a loaf of bread. I used the dough from the Basic Bread recipe (see page 22). When you have made the dough, just before it's ready to shape, pull a blob of it off – about 50 g/1¾ oz. or a blob the size of an apricot or a ping-pong ball.

1. Sprinkle a little flour on your hands and then roll the blob of dough between your palms until you get a sausage shape. The dough sausage needs to be thin enough to fit through the opening of your small bottle. Now feed the dough into the bottle so that it drops inside.

2. Take the balloon and blow it up about halfway, just to stretch it slightly. This will make it easier for it to expand later. Now let it deflate.

3 Stretch the opening of the balloon over the neck of the bottle so that it fits tightly over the hole and there are no gaps. After a little bit of time, small bubbles will start to appear on the surface of the dough.

4 Leave the bottle and balloon in a warmish place overnight. By the morning, the balloon will have filled with air, and the dough will be about 3 times bigger than when you first put it in!

5 Soon afterwards, the dough will have risen so much that many of the air bubbles in the dough burst, causing the balloon to shrink and deflate again.

So, what's going on inside the bottle to make the balloon inflate?

The cleverest part of breadmaking is the yeast. Yeast might look and smell a bit odd but this is probably because it's a living thing (a fungus, to be precise, but don't let that put you off!) and it likes to feed on sugar. So, when you mix it with flour and water, it converts the starch into simple sugars. (If you want to find out more about starch, see page 132.) Then it can start feeding! You know when you eat too quickly and a burp pops out?! Well the same thing happens when yeast gobbles up sugar – it burps carbon dioxide, creating little air bubbles in the dough. The gluten, which was created when you folded and kneaded the dough, is a little bit like bubble gum or elastic. This allows the bubbles in the dough to get bigger without bursting. As more and more of these bubbles are created in the dough, they help to make the dough rise. This expanding dough takes up valuable air space in the bottle and the air has nowhere left to go but inside the balloon, which is why it starts to blow up! Alcohol is also produced during this rising process, but don't worry – the bread that you make from the dough won't taste of beer or wine (!), but it does help to give the bread a nice flavour.

So why does the balloon start to deflate?

Imagine blowing a bubble of bubble gum or blowing up a balloon: if you blow too much air into it, it will eventually pop. So when the dough in your bottle starts to deflate and the balloon loses some of its shape, the gluten has been stretched too far and your precious air bubbles are starting to burst. The yeast has also stopped working.

Similar experiments

Yeast isn't the only thing that can cause dough to rise. Baking powder and bicarbonate of/baking soda both have a similar effect and are both often used to make breads, cakes, muffins and other baked goods. When water is mixed into baking powder or bicarbonate of/baking soda, a chemical reaction occurs that, exactly like the yeast on the opposite page, produces carbon dioxide in the form of air bubbles. However, this process happens a lot quicker (almost instantly) than it does with yeast, which takes 2–3 hours to produce the same reaction. This makes baking powder and bicarbonate of/baking soda more convenient. So why do we bother with yeast then? Well, yeast creates a distinctive aroma and flavour

that makes bread taste like bread. Bicarbonate of/baking soda and baking powder don't improve the flavour of the bread, so other products are needed in order to enhance it. Yeast also creates a distinctive texture during the rising process. The airy holes in the crust, for example, are caused by the yeast.

Mixing baking soda and water

So, what happens when we switch yeast for baking powder or bicarbonate of/baking soda? Instead of adding the dough to the bottle, try adding a tablespoon of bicarbonate of/baking soda to 250 ml/1 cup of warm water, carefully fix a balloon around the rim of the bottle again and see what happens. You can try the experiment again with really hot or really cold water and see how it affects the outcome.

Mixing baking soda and water with vinegar

For this experiment, you'll need a clean bottle (you can use the same one as for the experiment opposite but make sure to clean it), a clean balloon, a small plastic funnel, some cold water and some vinegar.

1 Add around 1.25 cm/½ in. of cold water with the same amount of vinegar to the bottle (make sure the bottle is clean first).

2 Then, take a balloon, stretch it a few times to make a little more elastic and use a funnel to half-fill the balloon with bicarbonate of/baking soda.

3 Carefully attach the balloon to the rim of the bottle, but make sure that none of the bicarbonate of/baking soda falls into the vinegar and water mixture yet.

4 When you're ready, move the balloon so it's directly over the liquid and the bicarbonate of/baking soda falls into it. Now watch the bubbles and what happens to the balloon!

 Fascinating Fact:

A small block of yeast is composed of a huge number of organisms, which can only be seen under a microscope. A 1 cm/⅓ in. cube of yeast weighs around 1 g/0.05 oz. and contains more than 10 billion living yeast cells!

60-minute Soda Bread

Ingredients:

400 g/3¼ cups white strong/bread flour, plus extra for coating

8 g/2 teaspoons salt

6 g/1 tablespoon bicarbonate of/ baking soda (sifted if lumpy)

300 g/300 ml/1¼ cups milk

Equipment:

wooden spoon

large mixing bowl

deep roasting tray

baking tray lined with parchment paper

plastic scraper

Makes 1 small loaf

This simple recipe is perfect if you want to make lovely hot, rustic bread as quickly as possible. It's also a great way to get acquainted with making bread. Try making this and you'll never pop down to the shops for a loaf of bread again!

1 Preheat your oven to 250°C (480°F) Gas 9. Place a deep roasting tray on the base of the oven.

2 Mix the flour, salt and bicarbonate of/baking soda in a large mixing bowl with a wooden spoon and set aside. **This is the dry mixture (A)**.

3 Mix the milk into the dry mixture, until it just comes together (**B**).

4 Scoop the mixture out of the mixing bowl using a plastic scraper and place it on the prepared baking tray. Generously sprinkle with flour (**C**).

5 Place the loaf on the prepared tray in the preheated oven and pour a cup of water to the hot roasting tray to form steam (**ask an adult to help you with this**). Lower the oven temperature to 200°C (390°F) Gas 6 and bake for 20–30 minutes.

6 Carefully remove the loaf from the oven using oven mitts (ask an adult to help you with this). Check that the loaf is baked by tapping it on the bottom with your knuckles. If you hear a hollow sound, it's ready!

7 Allow to cool on a wire rack before slicing it (**ask an adult to help you with this**).

Variation: If you want a neatly shaped loaf, you can bake the loaf in a 500–g/6 x 4-in. greased pan; if you want to do this follow steps 1–3 but add an extra 200 g/200 ml/¾ cup milk in step 2. Add the dough mixture to the prepared pan and follow the instructions above for baking the loaf.

A

B

Basic Bread

Now you've learned how to make 60-minute Soda Bread, you're ready to make bread with yeast, which will make the dough rise to form a beautiful, golden-crusted classic loaf. Once you've mastered this one, you'll be ready to experiment with the exciting recipes that follow.

Ingredients:

300 g/2⅓ cups white strong/bread flour plus extra for dusting

6 g/1 teaspoon salt

3 g fresh yeast or 2 g/¾ teaspoon dried/active dry yeast

200 g/200 ml/¾ cup warm water

Equipment:

2 small mixing bowls

measuring jug/pitcher

500-g/6 x 4-in. loaf pan, greased with vegetable oil

large mixing bowl

pastry brush, for greasing the tin

plastic scraper

Makes 1 small loaf

How to make the dough

1 In a small mixing bowl, mix the flour and salt and set aside. **This is the dry mixture (A).**

2 Weigh or measure out the water in the measuring jug/pitcher and transfer ¾ of it into your large mixing bowl.

3 Weigh out the yeast and add it to the large mixing bowl containing the water (**B**). **This is the wet mixture.** If you're using dried/active dry yeast, soak it for 10 minutes or until it floats to the top and bubbles. If you're using fresh yeast, dissolve it in warm water with your hands. If you're using instant/quick dry yeast or fast-acting yeast, **see page 17.**

4 Add the dry mixture to the wet mixture (**C**). Use your hands to scoop out any dry mixture remaining in the small mixing bowl.

5 Stir the mixture slowly with your hands until it comes together (**D**). If it doesn't come together and it seems a bit dry, add a little of the remaining water you weighed out in the measuring jug/pitcher in step 2. At this point the dough should come together and be slightly sticky.

6 Use a plastic scraper to scrape the sides of the bowl clean and make sure all the ingredients are thoroughly mixed together (**E**).

7 Cover the dough with the small mixing bowl that originally contained the flour. Leave the mixture to stand for 10 minutes. You'll then be ready to start kneading the dough (**F**).

Note: Different types of flour will absorb different amounts of water, so remember that you can always add water but never take it out. This is why I start with ¾ of the water in the beginning.

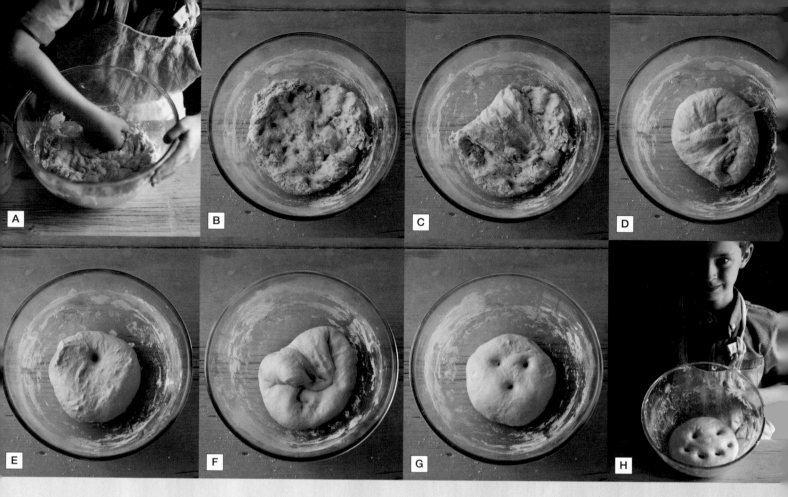

How to knead the dough

1 Squash the dough with your knuckles and fingers to flatten out any lumps (**A**). It should now look pancake-shaped (**B**).

2 Lift a portion of the dough up from the side and **fold** it into the middle (**C**)

3 Turn the bowl 90° clockwise and lift another portion of the dough up from the side and fold it into the middle.

4 Repeat step 3 **eight** times (remembering to turn the dough 90° each time) until you've **lifted and folded the dough 10 times**. You've now kneaded the dough once! (**D**)

5 Now turn the dough over. Wet your finger and make a fairly deep mark in the middle of the dough to show that you've kneaded the dough once (**E**).

6 Cover the dough with the small bowl that contained the flour and leave it to rest on your work surface for 10 minutes.

7 Repeat steps 2–6 three more times (picture **G** shows the dough after the third knead), so you will have kneaded the dough a total of **4 times**. Make sure to cover the mixture between kneads for 10 minutes and to mark the dough to remind you of the the number of times you've kneaded it. The dough should now be smooth and elastic. If not, you'll need to knead the dough once or twice more (**H**).

8 Once the dough is smooth and elastic, cover it with the small bowl again for 1 hour. This is really important, because if the dough is not covered a skin will form and this will affect your finished loaf.

9 As the dough rises, your finger marks will start to disappear from the surface of the dough (**I**). This is because the dough has got stronger and more elastic (see pages 130–131). After 1 hour, you'll be ready to start shaping your dough into a loaf!

How to shape the dough into a loaf

1 After 1 hour, the dough will have increased in volume. Clench your hand into a fist and **gently punch down** the centre of the dough to **release the trapped air** (**A**).

2 Transfer the dough to a lightly floured surface using a plastic scraper. If the dough is sticky, coat it in a little flour. Shape the dough into an oval and flatten the surface (**B**).

3 Take the right hand-side of the dough and fold it to the middle (**C**), then do the same with the left-hand side of the dough. The dough should now be square-shaped (**D**).

4 Take the top part of the square and elongate it so that the top of the dough becomes triangular (**E**).

5 Take the point of the "triangle" and fold it back over the dough to form a square again (**F**).

6 Use the tips of your fingers to straighten and tighten the top third of the dough and form it into a swiss/jelly-roll shape (**G**) (**H**).

7 Roll the top section over your finger marks and repeatedly straighten and tighten it to form a loaf-shape (**I**). If it doesn't fit in the pan, you'll need to follow **steps 8 and 9**.

8 Turn the loaf over so the seam running along the middle of the dough faces you. Rotate the dough 90° to the right (**J**).

9 Continue the straightening and tightening process again to form a wider, shorter loaf than you created in steps 6–7. This should now fit nicely into your loaf pan. (**K**) (**L**) (**M**) (**N**) (**O**)

A

B

C

D

E

F

How to get the loaf ready for baking

1 Pop the loaf seam-side down into the greased loaf pan (**A**) (**B**).

2 Cover it with a shower cap, (making sure that the top of the shower cap doesn't touch the dough) or a large mixing bowl that will fit completely over the pan.

3 If your kitchen is fairly warm, you can just leave the loaf pan (covered with the shower cap, or with the mixing bowl that you used to knead the dough in, so a skin doesn't form on the surface) as it is, to rise for about 30 minutes. **If your kitchen isn't that warm,** you'll need to preheat your oven to 50°C (110°F). Place a damp tea/dish towel on the shelf above the bottom of your oven. Now place the loaf pan on top of the damp tea/dish towel and **turn the oven off immediately**. Leave it to rise for about 30 minutes. If you don't turn the oven off, the bread will start to cook slowly, and we don't want that to happen yet!

4 Check the loaf after 15 minutes (and then 15 minutes after that) to see how it is rising. Once the dough has risen so that it is **level with the surface of the pan**, remove the loaf pan and the tea/dish towel from the oven.

A

C

5 **You can do a little test to see if the dough is ready for baking**: first remove the shower cap or mixing bowl and gently press your finger into the dough to make a small hole. If the hole **springs back** so that it looks like it did before you pushed your finger in, you'll need to leave the loaf pan on your work surface (if your kitchen is warm enough) or in the preheated oven again (if your kitchen isn't that warm) for a little bit longer. **If the finger mark doesn't spring back, it's ready to bake! (C)**

6 Lastly, cover the loaf with the shower cap or the large mixing bowl again (the one you used to knead the dough) to prevent a skin from forming.

B

How to bake the loaf

1 Preheat the oven to 250°C, (480°F) Gas 9 and place a deep roasting tray on the bottom shelf.

2 When the oven has heated to the right temperature, remove the large mixing bowl or shower cap and place the loaf pan in the baking tray.

3 Fill a cup with water and pour it into the hot baking tray (**ask an adult to help with this**) to create steam – this will help form a lovely crust.

4 Lower the oven temperature to 200°C (400°F) Gas 6 and bake the loaf for around **35 minutes** until golden brown.

5 Remove the loaf pan from the oven using oven mitts (**ask an adult to help with this**).

6 Carefully turn the loaf out of the loaf pan. To check if it is baked through, tap the bottom of the loaf with your knuckles – it should sound hollow (**A**). If not, you'll need to leave it in for a little longer.

7 Make sure the bread has cooled down before slicing it (**ask an adult to help with this**).

Variation: To create a thicker crust, remove the loaf pan from the oven after 35 minutes. Carefully take the loaf out of the pan. Lower the oven temperature to 180°C (350°F) Gas 4, and place the loaf directly on the middle oven shelf. Bake for another 10 minutes. Wait for the loaf to cool before slicing it.

Playdough

This is a great dough to experiment and have fun with, but it's not suitable for baking. It's versatile and pliable, so it's good for practising your kneading and shaping techniques. You can mould playdough into almost any shape you can imagine (well nearly!). I've suggested seven shapes here, but there's no end to what you can create with the dough if you put your mind to it!

Ingredients:

360 g/3 cups white strong/bread flour

15 g/2 tablespoons cream of tartar

30 g/2 tablespoons vegetable or sunflower oil

400 g/400 ml/1¾ cups water

180 g/1 cup salt

Equipment:

large mixing bowl

small saucepan

wooden spoon

plastic bucket/ container with lid

1 In a large mixing bowl, mix the flour, cream of tartar and the oil together.

2 Add the water and the salt to a small saucepan and heat over a medium heat (**ask an adult to help with this**). **This is the wet mixture.**

3 Once the salt has dissolved and the water starts to boil, turn off the heat and add the wet mixture to the flour mixture in the large mixing bowl.

4 Mix vigorously with a wooden spoon until it forms a dough. Allow the dough to cool.

5 Remove the dough from the bowl and knead it until it's soft and pliable (see page 24). **Ask an adult to help.**

6 You can now use the dough to make knots, plaits or spirals or anything you like! If you're not using the dough straight away, keep it in a **plastic bucket/container and cover it** so it doesn't dry out.

Fun Bread Rolls

For this recipe, you'll need to follow steps 1–6 of the Basic Bread recipe (page 22) but you'll need to double the amount of yeast. If you're unsure about how to roll the dough into a ball, see page 42.

1 With a light sprinkling of flour, divide the prepared dough into six 80 g/2.5 oz. portions using a scraper. You'll now mould the dough into 6 different shapes:

2 Roll the dough into a ball. Push your index finger through the centre of the dough. Push your other index finger through the

Ingredients:

1 tablespoon white strong/bread flour, plus extra for sprinkling

1 tablespoon sesame seeds

1 tablespoon wholemeal/whole-wheat flour

1 tablespoon porridge/steel-cut oats

1 tablespoon semolina flour

Equipment:

plastic scraper

pastry brush

baking tray lined with parchment paper

large mixing bowl

deep roasting tray

Makes 6 rolls

A   B   C

D   E   F

other side and widen the hole by rotating the ball of dough (**A**).

3 Roll the dough into a 25 cm/10 in. sausage. Pick up the left-hand side and wrap it under the right-hand side and then under to form a simple knot. Sprinkle with sesame seeds (**B**).

4 Roll the dough into a 25 cm/10 in. sausage with the ends slightly pointed. Coil it into a snail-shell shape and tuck the end underneath. Sprinkle with the white strong/bread flour. (**C**)

5 Roll the dough into a thick sausage, then form it into a horseshoe shape. Take the right-hand side and fold it over the left-hand side. Pinch the ends together and then sprinkle with wholemeal/whole-wheat flour (**D**).

6 Roll the dough into a thick sausage and then fold it back on itself so it forms an 'N' shape. Sprinkle oats on top. (**E**).

7 Roll the dough into a ball. Dip the smooth side in semolina flour and flatten the dough with the palm of your hand. Take the left-hand side, fold it into the middle, then take the right hand side and fold it into the middle (**F**).

8 Place the rolls onto the baking tray and cover with the mixing bowl. Let the rolls rise until they have almost **doubled in size** (15–20 minutes). After 10 minutes, preheat the oven to 250°C (480°F) Gas 9 and place the roasting tray on the base. Place the baking tray inside the roasting tray in the oven and pour a cup of water into the hot roasting tray (**ask an adult to help with this**). Then lower the oven temperature to 200°C (400°F) Gas 6. Bake for around 15 minutes until they've turned golden brown!

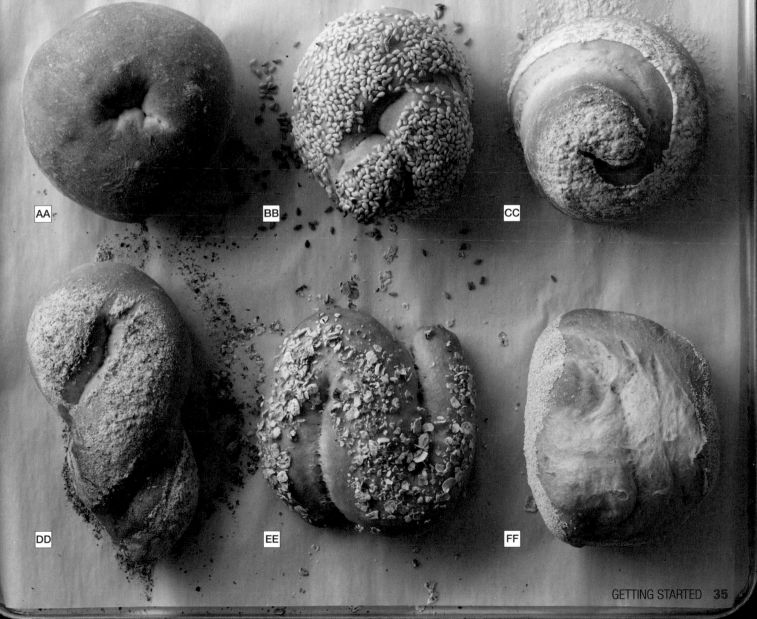

AA BB CC

DD EE FF

How to Make a Sourdough "Starter"

Sourdough, or wild yeast, is a type of yeast that is used to make bread and other yeast related products. It takes 5 days to make a fully active sourdough 'starter' and you can use many different kinds of flour to make it. It also requires feeding (refreshing) to keep it going!

Hundreds of years ago, before packaged yeast had been invented, bakers used to keep a pot of live culture made of a flour and water mixture, and 'fed' it daily or weekly to keep it alive and active. Today, this is known as a "sourdough starter" or wild yeast.

Making your own sourdough 'starter' is very easy, and it's quite similar to looking after a pet! Sourdough needs to be fed, or refreshed, to keep it happy and when you're not using it, it's happy to go to sleep (in the refrigerator!).

Just Two Ingredients

To create your own natural yeast, you'll need 1 teaspoon of flour, 1–2 teaspoons of water and a container that can be sealed, like a clean miniature jam/jelly jar. Alternatively, you can use a larger jar like a kilner jar.

As for the type of flour, you can use most types to make sourdough. However, don't use self-raising/rising flour, as it contains a chemical that makes the dough rise already, and you'll want the sourdough to rise without any additional help! I wouldn't use bleached flour as all the natural goodness (in my opinion, anyway!) has been taken out. I tend to use organic flour because it doesn't contain any chemicals that will affect or even kill the sourdough. I find that rye flour (particularly light rye, which is grey in colour) works very well because you can use it for rye bread, wheat bread, spelt bread and any other bread using a grain that has gluten in it. Remember not to use it for gluten-free products as rye contains gluten.

As for the water, I always say if you can't drink the water, then neither should the sourdough starter! So to be on the safe side, start with bottled water. I also use hand warm water, as cold water will slow it down. Ideally, you're looking for a temperature of between 30°C (86°F)–37°C (99°F).

Use Your Nose

Make sure you smell your mixture often, as it will change during the fermentation process. You will notice a big difference by day 3 and the batter should start to bubble. The smells you will get are grass smells, maybe a cheesy smell, and definitely a vinegary smell. It might smell a little alcoholic or like nail polish remover, too. Don't worry – all these smells are a good sign! If you notice a foul smell, don't worry – as long as there are bubbles in the mixture, it is working!

Different types of Sourdough

If you make two different sourdough starters with two different types of flour, for example one with white flour and one with rye flour, you will notice a few different things. The rye mixture might take more water than the white flour one. Also the white one will be more elastic than the rye one. This is because wheat flour contains more gluten than rye flour.

The mixture you have made up over the 5 days is normally called your "**Mother**" or "**Chef**". You now need to build your Mother or Chef up so you have enough for your bread and a little left over for the next time.

To make your 'Mother' or 'Chef' mixture:

Day 1 In a clean jar, mix together 1 level teaspoon of flour and 1–2 level teaspoons of water with your chosen wooden stick. Seal the jar and leave to stand overnight in a warm place.

Day 2 Add another 1 teaspoon of flour and 1–2 teaspoons of water to the mixture. Now smell the mixture. It should smell just like flour and water mixed together, depending on what type of flour you've used. Its consistency should be that of a thick-ish batter. If the mixture is too soft add less water next time. Reseal the jar and leave to stand overnight in a warm place again.

Day 3 Repeat the instructions from Day 2 again, leaving it in a warm place overnight.

Day 4 Repeat the instructions from Day 2 again, leaving it in a warm place overnight. There should be little bubbles forming in the mixture and it should have a slight vinegary smell, or it might smell like nail polish remover.

Day 5 (part 1) The mixture is now bubbling nicely, so it's ready to use. If it's not bubbling like it is in the image (left), add another 1 teaspoon of flour and 1–2 teaspoons of water and check it the next day.

Day 5 (part 2) Now build up your sourdough. Put the sourdough starter into a large mixing bowl, and add 100 g/1 scant cup dark rye flour (if you've made a rye sourdough starter) or 100 g/¾ cup white flour (if you've made a white sourdough starter). Add 100 g/100 ml/⅓ cup warm water to the large mixing bowl and mix together.

Cover the bowl with a shower cap and leave to ferment overnight in a warm place.

Day 6 The next day, you can start making your sourdough recipe. Take whatever quantity of sourdough starter is needed (eg 150 g/⅔ cup, if you want to make the **Half-and-half Sourdough Loaf on page 41**) and put the rest back in the jam/jelly jar or kilner jar.

Add 1–2 teaspoons of flour and about 2 teaspoons of water (to make it into a thick batter) to the mixture in the jam/jelly jar or kilner jar. Place the jam/jelly jar or kilner jar in the refrigerator until you're ready to build it up again (following the instructions on pages 36–38) for the next bread!

Bringing your pet sourdough starter back to life

What happens if you don't make bread using your sourdough starter for a while and it's been in the refrigerator for a long time? Well the coldness of the refrigerator slows down the process of fermentation and the **mixture goes to sleep**. Don't worry – this doesn't mean it's dead!

You may also find that it will have separated and a grey/brown liquid might form on top. It'll probably have quite a strong vinegar smell but it's safe to taste (**but only if you're brave, because it will be very sour!**) Your sourdough starter may look like it can't be saved, but don't worry – it can! **First, carefully pour away the brown liquid.** Never mix it in as it will get very sour and take a long time to come back to life! Now begin building it up slowly, following the instructions on the top left of this page. However, start by adding just 5 g/5 ml of the mixture from the jar and 50 g/scant ½ cup of dark rye flour (for a rye sourdough starter) or 50 g/6 tablespoons white flour (for a white sourdough starter) and 50 g/50 ml/3½ tablespoons of water. Leave it in a warm place to bubble. If it's not bubbling when you check it the next day, add the same quantity of flour and water again and leave it in a warm place again overnight. Keep on doing this until it is bubbling. When it is – it's ready to use again. **Remember that if your sourdough is not bubbling your bread will not rise!**

Half-and-half Sourdough Loaf

Ingredients:
150 g/⅔ cup white sourdough starter (see pages 36–38)

300 g/300 ml/1¼ cups water, warm

250 g/2 cups white strong/bread flour, plus extra for dusting

250 g/2 cups wholemeal/whole-wheat flour

8 g/2 teaspoons salt

250 g/2½ cups wheat bran, for coating

Equipment:
large mixing bowl

measuring jug/pitcher

small mixing bowl

shower cap (optional)

plastic scraper

round 500-g/1-lb. proofing/dough-rising basket

1 deep roasting tray

small peel (for transferring the loaf into the oven)

Makes 1 loaf

You've now learned all about sourdough, so you're ready to make your first sourdough loaf. It contains 50 per cent wholemeal/whole-wheat flour and 50 per cent white strong/bread flour, so it's lighter than a dense 100 per cent wholemeal loaf, but it's still good for you. A perfect balance!

1 Weigh out the sourdough starter in a large mixing bowl.

2 Measure the water in a measuring jug/pitcher and add ¾ of it to the sourdough starter (**A**). Set the remaining ¼ of the water aside.

3 Use your hands to help dissolve the sourdough starter (**B**).

4 In a small mixing bowl, mix the flour and salt together thoroughly and set aside. This is the **dry mixture**.

5 Once the sourdough has dissolved, **add the dry mixture to the dissolved sourdough** (**C**).

6 Mix together the dissolved sourdough and dry mixture using your hands until it forms a rough dough (**D**). If it doesn't quite come together, add a little or all of the remaining water. Cover the mixture with the small bowl that contained the dry mixture or a shower cap and leave it to stand for 10 minutes.

A   B   C   D

7 Remove the upturned mixing bowl or shower cap.

8 In the large mixing bowl, lift a portion of the dough up from the side and fold it back into the middle of the dough (**E**).

9 Turn the bowl 90° clockwise and repeat the lifting and folding process until you've done it 10 times. Turn the ball of dough over in the bowl and make a finger mark in it (to indicate the first complete knead) (**F**).

10 Cover with the smaller mixing bowl. Leave the dough to rest for 10 minutes.

11 Repeat steps 8, 9 and 10 another **3 times**. After you have done 4 complete kneads, the dough should be smooth and elastic. If not, you'll need to knead the dough once or twice more. Picture **G** shows 7 finger marks in the dough, but that's because she's kneaded it 4 times and added 3 finger marks to make a smiley face!

12 Once the dough is smooth and elastic, leave it to rise for 1 hour and cover it with the small mixing bowl or a shower cap.

13 After an hour, the dough will have increased in volume (**H**).

14 Clench you hand into a fist and **gently punch down the centre** of the dough to release the trapped air.

15 Lightly flour the work surface so that the dough doesn't stick. Remove the dough from the bowl using a plastic scraper and place the dough on the floured work surface (**I**).

16 Shape the ball of dough into a rounded loaf: first, flatten the dough slightly with your palm (**J**).

17 Take a corner of the dough and fold it right over to the opposite side (**K**). Turn the dough 90° clockwise.

18 Repeat step **17** four to five more times and then turn the dough over.

19 Tuck in the underneath of the dough with your fingers as you rotate the dough clockwise until you've formed a rounded ball (**L**) (**M**).

E F G H

I J K L

20 Coat the top of the dough liberally with the wheat bran.

21 Prepare a proofing/dough-rising basket by sprinkling it liberally with wheat bran. Transfer the dough to the basket (**N**). You may need to stretch the dough so that it its snugly in the basket without a gap around the edge.

22 Sprinkle the dough with a couple of handfuls of the wheat bran (**O**).

23 Next, leave the dough until it has **doubled in size**. This will take 3–6 hours. If your kitchen is fairly warm, leave the dough in the proofing basket (covered with the shower cap or bowl) to rise. If your kitchen isn't that warm, follow the instructions on **page 28**, but let the dough rise for 3–6 hours.

24 Remove the shower cap or bowl and place the dough (still in the proofing basket) in the fridge for 30 minutes to stabilize it so that it doesn't spread like a pancake on the peel/board.

25 Preheat your oven to 250°C (480°F) Gas 9 and place a deep roasting tray on the bottom shelf.

26 After 30 minutes in the fridge, turn the dough out onto a lightly floured peel/board (**P**).

27 Add a decoration to the top of the dough, by pushing a clean finger into it to create a pattern (**Q**).

28 Place the loaf in the preheated oven and pour a cup of water into the hot tray (**ask an adult to help**). Lower the oven temperature to 220°C (425°F) Gas 7. Bake for 30–40 minutes until golden brown and allow to cool before slicing.

breakfast

Muesli Bread

This has got everything you could want in a nutritious breakfast, and all in one place, too. It's one of the most satisfying breads to cut into, as you can see all the fruit, nuts and seeds dotted inside the bread. It's great with a little honey. For this recipe, you'll need to prepare the pre-ferment a day in advance of making the bread.

Ingredients:

150 g/1 heaping cup dark rye flour

100 g/scant ½ cup rye or white sourdough starter (see pages 36–38)

200 g/200 ml/¾ cup water, warm

60 g/⅔ cup wholegrain oat flakes/jumbo rolled oats

25 g/3 tablespoons raisins

20 g/2 tablespoons sunflower seeds

20 g/2 tablespoons pumpkin seeds/pepitas

20 g/3 tablespoons coconut chips

20 g/2 tablespoons whole almonds

20 g/2 tablespoons toasted whole hazelnuts

15 g/2 tablespoons golden linseed/flaxseed

70 g/⅔ cup wholemeal/whole-wheat flour

4 g/1 teaspoon salt

30 g/2 tablespoons honey

100 g/100 ml/scant ½ cup water, hot (from the kettle)

porridge/steel-cut oats, for topping

Equipment:

2 large mixing bowls

wooden spoon

plastic scraper

3 small mixing bowls

shower cap (optional)

pastry brush, for greasing the loaf pan

500-g/6 x 4-in. loaf pan, greased with vegetable or sunflower oil

deep roasting tray

Makes 1 loaf

A

B

1 **The day before you make the bread**, you need to prepare the **pre-ferment**. To do this, add the dark rye flour, the rye or white sourdough starter and the warm water to a large mixing bowl and mix well with a wooden spoon. (**A**). Use the plastic scraper to scrape down the sides of the bowl to stop the mixture sticking and drying out. Leave the mixture to ferment overnight covered with an upturned small mixing bowl or a shower cap. **This is the wet mixture.**

2 **To make the muesli**, add the wholegrain oat flakes/jumbo rolled oats, raisins, sunflower seeds, pumpkin seeds/pepitas, coconut chips, almonds, toasted hazelnuts and the golden linseed/flaxseed together in a large mixing bowl (**B**).

3 In a small mixing bowl, mix the wholemeal/whole-wheat flour and salt.

4 Add the muesli mixture to the flour and salt mixture. **This is the dry mixture (C)**.

5 Tip the dry mixture into the pre-ferment (D). **This is the wet mixture**.

6 In the last small bowl, dissolve the honey in the hot water (E).

7 Add the the **hot honey mixture** to the **wet mixture** and mix thoroughly with a wooden spoon (F).

8 Spoon the mixture into the prepared loaf pan (G).

9 Level the mixture using the wooden spoon or a plastic scraper dipped in a little water (**H**).

10 Sprinkle some of the porridge/steel-cut oats on the surface for decoration (**I**).

11 Cover the loaf pan with a large mixing bowl or a shower cap and, if your kitchen is fairly warm, you can leave the dough to rise (proof) for around 2 hours. If your kitchen isn't that warm, **follow the instructions on page 28**, but leave the dough in the oven for **2 hours** rather than 30 minutes.

12 After about 1½ hours, preheat your oven to 250°C (480°F) Gas 9; and place a deep roasting tray at the bottom. **Remember to remove the loaf pan from the oven if you left it to rise there**!

13 The loaf is ready to bake when it rises to the top of the pan and when cracks and little air holes appear on the surface (**J**).

14 When the loaf is ready to bake, remove the bowl or shower cap that has been covering it and place the pan in the preheated oven.

15 Pour a cup of water into the hot roasting tray (**ask an adult to help with this**) and then lower the oven temperature to 220°C (425°F) Gas 7.

16 Bake for around 40 minutes until golden brown. Carefully turn out the loaf from the pan. Let the bread cool on a wire rack before slicing and enjoying it! (**K**)

Sourdough Scotch Pancakes

These pancakes are a great breakfast option and are really versatile, as they are delicious with savoury or sweet toppings. Why not enjoy them with a dollop of butter, fresh fruit or maple syrup, or maybe a little of all three!

Ingredients:

50 g/scant ¼ cup white or rye sourdough starter (see pages 36–39)

250 g/250 ml/1 cup whole milk or water

250 g/2 cups white strong/bread flour

25 g/⅛ cup sugar

3 g/¾ teaspoon salt

6 g/1½ teaspoons baking powder

120 g/120 ml/½ cup water, cold

Equipment:

large mixing bowl

balloon whisk

small mixing bowl

shower cap (optional)

griddle, hot-plate or heavy-based frying pan, greased

ladle or large spoon

spatula or palette knife

Makes 15

1 In a large mixing bowl, dissolve the sourdough starter in the milk or water. **This is the wet mixture**.

2 Add the flour, sugar and salt to the wet mixture and beat vigorously using a balloon whisk until it forms a smooth, thick batter.

3 Cover the mixture with an upturned small mixing bowl or a shower cap and leave to rise overnight in a warm place. If your kitchen isn't that warm, **follow the instructions on page 28**, but leave the dough in the oven **overnight rather than 30 minutes**. **The next day** the mixture should be bubbling nicely.

4 In the small mixing bowl dissolve the baking powder in the 120 g/120 ml/½ cup water and add it to the mixture in the large bowl (**A**). Make sure that it's mixed thoroughly in (**B**).

5 To cook the pancakes, lightly grease a griddle, hot-plate or heavy-based frying pan and heat until a drop of batter sizzles immediately on contact (**ask an adult to help you with this**).

6 Cook the pancakes in batches by using a ladle or a large spoon to drop 3–4 small quantities of batter on the hot surface. Each pancake should spread to about 10 cm/4 inches in diameter; you might have to tilt the pan to help them spread.

7 Cook them until the top of each pancake is no longer wet. Turn each pancake over with a thin spatula or palette knife and cook the other side until it is lightly browned.

8 Serve either hot from the pan or keep the pancakes warm by stacking them, covering them with foil and eating them soon afterwards!

Gluten-free Potato and Raspberry Swirl Bread

With the swirl of raspberry running through it, this bread not only looks great, but it also keeps the bread nice and moist. It's a great breakfast bread, particularly with a little butter and a lovely dollop of sticky jam/jelly on top.

Ingredients:

8 g fresh yeast or
4 g/1 teaspoon
dried/active dry
yeast

170 g/170 ml/⅔ cup
water, warm

150 g/1 cup potato
starch

150 g/1 cup
gram/chickpea flour

4 g/¾ teaspoon salt

150 g/1 heaping cup
potatoes (with skin
on or peeled), finely
grated

100 g/⅓ cup
raspberry jam/jelly

Equipment:

large mixing bowl

2 small mixing bowls

wooden spoon

cheese grater

ladle

*500-g/6 x 4-in. loaf
pan, greased with
vegetable oil*

*pastry brush, for
greasing the pan*

*clean chopstick or
wooden skewer*

shower cap

deep roasting tray

Makes 1 loaf

1 In the large mixing bowl dissolve or activate the yeast in the warm water (**see step 3 on page 22,** unless you're using instant/quick dry or fast-acting yeast, in which case **see page 17**). **This is the wet mixture (A).**

2 In one of the small bowls, weigh out the potato starch, gram/chickpea flour and salt together and set aside. **This is the dry mixture (B).**

3 In another small bowl, grate the potato finely and add it, along with the dry mixture to the wet mixture (**C**). Remember not to grate the potato too far in advance, as it will discolour. Don't worry if you do, because it won't affect the taste of the bread once it's been baked.

4 Mix all the ingredients together thoroughly with the wooden spoon until it forms a batter (**D**).

Note: The lack of gluten in this recipe means that the mixture will be a batter consistency (a bit like a soft yoghurt), which can't be kneaded. The yeast still produces air bubbles, though, which makes the bread rise.

5 Once you've mixed it into a batter, cover it with the bowl that contained the dry mixture and allow it to rise for 1 hour (**E**).

6 Remove the upturned bowl. After 1 hour, the batter will have increased in volume, and little air bubbles will have formed on the surface (**F**).

7 Stir the mixture vigorously (**G**) (**H**).

8 Spoon ⅓ of the mixture into the prepared loaf pan. Next, spoon a number of dollops of fruit jam/jelly on top of the batter to form a layer (**I**).

10 Place another ⅓ of the batter on top of the jam/jelly layer. Spoon another layer of jam/jelly onto the mixture before covering with the final third of batter (**J**).

11 Make a few swirls through the mixture with a clean chopstick or a wooden skewer (**K**).

12 Cover the pan with a shower cap and, if your kitchen is fairly warm, you can leave the batter to rise (proof) for around 30 minutes until it just reaches the top of the pan (**L**). If your kitchen isn't that warm, **follow the instructions on page 28**, and check after 15 minutes to see how it's rising.

13 Preheat the oven to 250°C (480°F) Gas 9, **remembering to remove the loaf pan if you left it to rise in there**! Cover the loaf pan with a shower cap or mixing bowl while the oven comes to temperature. Place a deep roasting tray on the bottom surface of the oven.

14 Place the loaf pan in the preheated oven and pour a cup of water into the hot roasting tray to form steam (**ask an adult to help with this**).

15 Lower the oven temperature to 220°C (425°F) Gas 7.

16 Bake for approximately 35 minutes until golden brown.

17 Carefully turn out the loaf from the pan. You'll know that it's baked when it makes a hollow sound when you tap it on the bottom (but be careful, because it'll be hot!). Allow the bread to cool on a wire rack before slicing it.

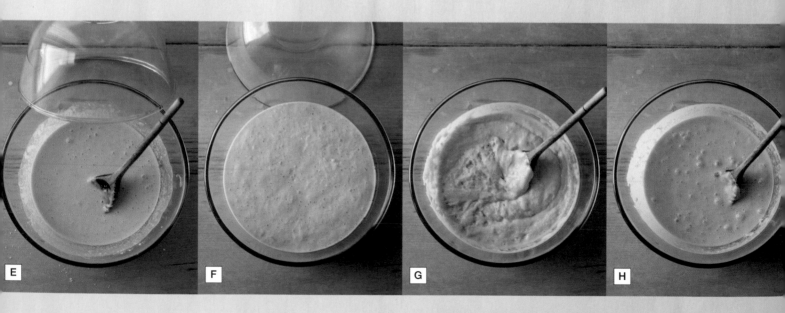

E   F   G   H

lunches and lunchboxes

Sunday Sandwich Loaf

**So-called because, traditionally, people are supposed to have
a bit more time on a Sunday! It's a good day to start making
this loaf, as it needs to rise overnight. Bake it the next day for
a perfect lunch-time loaf that's also great for your favourite
toasted sandwich.**

Ingredients:

750 g/5⅓ cups white strong/bread flour, plus extra for dusting

12 g/3 teaspoons salt

450 g/450 ml/1¼ cups water, warm

3 g fresh yeast or 1.5 g/¼ teaspoon dried/active dry yeast

135 g/1 cup sesame seeds

Equipment:

2 small mixing bowls

measuring jug/pitcher

large mixing bowl

shower cap (optional)

2 large plastic trays

pastry brush, for greasing the pan

1-kg/2-lbs. loaf pan, greased with vegetable oil

baking sheet, to cover the loaf

deep roasting tray

Makes 1 large loaf

1 In one of the smaller mixing bowls mix the flour and salt together thoroughly and set aside. This is the **dry mixture.**

2 Weigh out the water in the jug/pitcher and transfer ¾ of it into your large mixing bowl.

3 Weigh out the yeast and add it to the water. If you're using dried/active dry yeast, soak it for 10 minutes or until it floats to the top and bubbles. If you're using fresh yeast, dissolve it in warm water with your hands. If you're using instant/quick dry yeast or fast-acting yeast, **see page 17.**

4 Once the yeast has dissolved or activated, add the dry mixture to the yeast mixture

5 Stir the mixture slowly with your hands until it comes together. If it doesn't, add a little or all of the remaining water. At this point the dough should be slightly sticky.

6 Cover the mixture with the bowl that contained the dry mixture and leave to stand for 10 minutes.

7 Squash the dough in the bowl with your knuckles and fingers to flatten out any lumps. It should now look pancake-shaped.

8 **Lift** a portion of the dough up from one side and **fold** it into the middle. Turn the bowl 90° clockwise.

9 Repeat step 8 **nine** times until you've **lifted and folded the dough a total of 10 times**. You've now kneaded the dough once.

10 Now turn the dough over. Wet your finger and make a deep mark in the middle of the dough to show that you've kneaded the dough once.

11 Cover the dough with the small bowl (or the shower cap) again and leave it to rest on your work surface for 10 minutes.

12 Repeat steps 8–11 **three more times**, so you will have kneaded the dough a total of **4 times.** The dough should now be smooth and elastic. If not, you'll need to knead the dough once or twice more.

13 Once the dough is smooth and elastic (the dough will be slightly stiffer than the Basic Bread dough on page 24), cover it with the smaller bowl

again (or the shower cap) but now **leave it to rise overnight.**

14 **The next day**, the dough will have increased in volume, so gently punch down the dough to release the trapped air.

15 On a lightly floured surface, shape the dough into a loaf (**see pages 26–27**).

16 Sprinkle the sesame seeds onto a large plastic tray. Place a damp tea/dish towel on another plastic tray. Roll the loaf on the towel and then into the seeds so it has an even covering all over (**A**, over the page). Place the loaf seam-side down into the loaf pan.

17 Cover the loaf pan with a baking sheet (**B**, over the page). **If your kitchen is fairly warm**, you can just leave the loaf pan to rise for about 1 hour.

If your kitchen isn't that warm, you'll need to follow the instructions on page 28, but check the loaf after **15–30 minutes** (and 15 minutes after that) to see how it is rising.

18 Once the dough has risen so that the baking sheet is lifted about 2 cm/¾ in. above the surface of the pan (**C**, over the page), it's ready for baking.

19 Before preheating the oven for baking, put the loaf pan in the oven and position another oven rack or tray about 4 cm/1½ in. above the surface of the loaf pan. This is important so that when the bread rises during baking, it is wedged between the racks or trays above and beneath the loaf pan. This will ensure that the bread has a flat top.

20 Preheat the oven to 250°C (500°F) Gas 9 and place a deep roasting tray on the bottom surface.

21 Place the loaf pan between the 2 oven racks or trays in the oven. Add a cup of water to the hot roasting tray at the bottom of the oven to form steam (**ask an adult to help with this**). Then, lower the oven temperature to 200°C (400°F) Gas 6.

22 Bake for 35–50 minutes until golden brown. Remove the pan from the oven using oven mitts. Carefully turn the loaf out of the loaf pan. Make sure the bread has cooled down before slicing it (**ask an adult to help with this**).

A

B

C

Wheat – the grass that changed the world

Wheat is a member of the group of plants grown all over the world which produce the edible seeds ("grain") that we call "cereals". Cereal is also the name given to many of the foods made from these grains, particularly those we like to eat at breakfast!

First harvested and sown by humans around 9,000 BC in what is now a small region of southeastern Turkey, wheat is now cultivated worldwide. Wheat is a special type of grass. Like all plants, it grows, flowers and produces seeds, but it's the seeds, or grains of wheat that are so special, because they're used in so many foods that we eat every day. The grains of wheat are separated from the inedible part, and are then ground into the fine powder we call "flour" (see pages 14–15).

Wheat grass, the young grass of the wheat plant, can even be used to make a drink which is full of vitamins and minerals. However, not all wheat is suitable for either making flour or for us to eat, and this goes to make other products such as animal feed and, amazingly, biofuel that can be used to power engines!

Farmers grow many types of wheat today, some of which have been specially developed for high levels of production and ease of harvesting. However, some specialist farmers still grow the old varieties of wheat, such as spelt, einkorn, kamut and emmer, known as "ancient grains". These tend to grow much higher than modern varieties and were useful in ancient times as the long stems could be used to thatch roofs and keep buildings watertight.

Wheat is typically planted in spring or winter, and is then harvested in the late summer or early autumn/fall. There are three different components of the harvesting process – reaping, threshing and winnowing. Reaping is the process of cutting (usually involving a long bladed tool like a scythe, see bottom right image on opposite page) and then collecting the wheat; threshing involves loosening the edible portion of the cereal grain from the protective casing ("chaff") that surrounds it. Winnowing is the process of separating the grain from the chaff. All three of these processes have been performed by humans for centuries, but these days, the vast majority of crops are harvested by machines, like combine harvesters. This specific machine gets its name from the fact that it performs the three components of the harvesting process at once. The development of such machines completely transformed crop production in the early 20th century. Modern advances have now seen features like laser-guided hydraulic steering and GPS tracking to make the process even more efficient and precise.

As an experiment, try to get some wheat grains to plant and see how they grow. You could speak nicely to a farmer who grows wheat and see if they will give you some wheat grains. Alternatively, you might be able to get some from your local pet shop. It is fun and exciting to watch it grow from a seed to a full-sized plant.

Fascinating Fact:

As well as breakfast cereals, wheat is a vital ingredient in bread, cakes, biscuits/cookies, pizza, pasta, noodles, muesli, pancakes, pies, pastries, muffins and doughnuts. It can also be used to make a number of alcoholic drinks, most commonly beer.

Ciabatta Family

This recipe does take a little time, but it really is worth it when you see your finished ciabatta family! You can also make a whole loaf if you like.
"Ciabatta" is Italian for "slipper". If you make the whole loaf, you'll see why!

B

C

D

Ingredients:

200 g/1⅔ white strong/bread flour or Italian "00" bread-making flour, plus extra for dusting

4 g/1 teaspoon salt

2 g fresh yeast or 1g/¼ teaspoon dried/active dry yeast

160 g/160 ml/⅔ cup water, warm

15 g/15 ml/ 1 tablespoon olive oil, for folding, plus extra to stop your fingers sticking

Equipment:

small mixing bowl

2 large mixing bowls

shower cap (optional)

stainless steel gingerbread family cookie cutters

baking tray lined with parchment paper

small peel (optional)

baking stone (optional)

Makes 1 loaf or a small ciabatta family

1 In the small mixing bowl, mix the flour and salt together and set aside. This is the **dry mixture**.

2 In one of the large mixing bowls, dissolve or activate the yeast in the warm water (unless you're using instant/quick dry yeast or fast-acting yeast, in which case **see page 17**). This is the **wet mixture**.

3 Add the dry mixture to the wet mixture. Mix it together into a sticky dough, making sure all the flour is mixed into the liquid.

4 Put the olive oil in the other large mixing bowl.

5 Place the sticky dough in the olive oil and allow it to rest for 1 hour, covered with an upturned small bowl (the bowl that contained the dry mixture) or a shower cap (**A**).

6 After 1 hour, it will have increased in volume (**B**).

7 Lightly fold the dough twice. Do this by taking the top part of the dough and pulling it to the middle, then take the left-hand side of the dough and pull it to the middle (**C**).

8 Rotate the bowl 180°, then take the top part of the dough and pull it to the middle again.

9 Rotate the bowl 90° clockwise, take the top part of the dough and pull it to the middle again.

10 Rotate the bowl 180°, take the top part of the dough and pull it to the middle again. Now turn the dough over.

11 Repeat steps 7–10 another **3 times**, but allow the dough to rest for 1 hour after each time,

covered with the small mixing bowl or a shower cap (**D**). If the dough is not covered a skin will form and this will affect the end result. If the dough sticks to the bowl, add a litle olive oil.

To make the ciabatta family, follow the instructions on the next page.

12 **To make a ciabatta loaf,** apply flour to your hands, then mould the dough into a slipper-shape: first tip the dough onto a generously floured work surface. Pull the top part of the dough to the middle, then fold the bottom part of the dough into the middle.

13 Lightly flour the dough. Turn it over and add more flour to the top. Tuck your hands under the dough to pick it up and then stretch the dough slightly by gently pulling your hands apart. The dough should now be rectangle-shaped.

14 Transfer the dough to your prepared baking tray and allow the loaf to rest for 10–15 minutes. Meanwhile, preheat your oven to 250°C (480°F) Gas 9.

15 Bake for about 15 minutes. (**Ciabatta does not need to be baked for long because you want a nice soft loaf with a thin crust**.)

16 Carefully remove the loaf from the baking tray. To check if it is baked through, tap the bottom of the loaf with your knuckles – it should sound hollow. Make sure the bread has cooled down before slicing it (**ask an adult to help with this**).

12A To make the ciabatta people, generously flour a work surface and place the ball of dough on it. Add flour to the dough's surface.

13A Place the four gingerbread cutters in a line above the dough, so you know how wide the dough needs to be.

14A Now, flatten the dough with your hands and gently press it with your fingers to elongate it.

15A Once it's wide and long enough, use the four cookie cutters to cut out the different shapes, making sure that there is a space between each one. **Ask an adult to help with this as you'll need to press firmly and move the cutters from side to side** to make sure they are cut all the way through.

16A Roll the figures and the remaining dough in flour (**E**) (**F**).

17A Place the figures and the rest of the dough onto the prepared baking tray. Preheat an oven to 250°C (480°F) Gas 9.

18A Bake in the preheated oven for about 15 minutes until they've turned golden brown (**G**) (**H**). Use oven mitts to remove the baking tray and transfer the shapes and the rest of the loaf to a wire rack to cool before enjoying them!

Ingredients to make the pre-ferment:

150 g/1 heaping cup dark rye flour, plus extra for sprinkling

100 g/scant ½ cup rye sourdough starter (see pages 36–38)

200 g/200 ml/¾ cup water, warm

Ingredients to make the dough:

500 g/3¼ cups red onion, thinly sliced

200 g/1½ cups dark rye flour

6 g/1½ teaspoons salt

150 g/150 ml/⅔ cup water, hot from the kettle

Equipment:

3 large mixing bowls

wooden spoon

small mixing bowl

shower cap (optional)

plastic scraper

baking tray lined with parchment paper

pastry brush, for greasing the pan

500-g/6 x 4-in. loaf pan, greased with vegetable oil

metal spoon (optional)

Makes 1 loaf

A

Caramelised Onion Rye Bread

This rich rye loaf made with caramelized onion is sweet and sour at the same time. It's wheat-free and makes a fantastic addition to a Ploughmans' Lunch, an old English meal featuring bread, cheese and chutney – a classic combination to keep farm workers going until dinner. Bear in mind that you will need to prepare the pre-ferment for this recipe a day before making the bread.

1 Gather together your ingredients for the pre-ferment (**A**).

2 In the first large mixing bowl, mix the dark rye flour, sourdough starter and warm water together thoroughly with a wooden spoon.

3 Leave the mixture to ferment overnight covered with an upturned small mixing bowl or a shower cap.

4 Scrape down the sides of the bowl using a plastic scraper so the mixture does not dry out. **This is the pre-ferment (the wet mixture).**

5 Place the sliced red onion onto the baking tray and dry in the oven at 150°C (300°F) Gas 2 until nice and crisp, then set aside (**B**). Don't worry if a few of the slices get a bit dark this will just add to the flavour.

6 On day 2, remove the lid from the pre-ferment. It should have risen overnight and will be dotted with little bubble holes (**C**).

7 In the second large mixing bowl, mix the dark rye flour, the salt and the onion.

B

C

D

E

F

G

H

I

8 Add the flour, onion and salt mixture to the **wet mixture** (pre-ferment), making sure that the pre-ferment is completely covered (**D**).

9 Add the hot water (**E**). **It's important to add the hot water last, as putting it directly onto the pre-ferment could harm the sourdough starter, meaning that your bread won't rise.**

10 Mix thoroughly with a wooden spoon until everything is combined. It should have a kind of porridge/oatmeal consistency (**F**).

11 Spoon the mixture into the prepared loaf pan (**G**). Dip the spoon in a little water if necessary so that the mixture does not stick to it.

12 Level the top of the mixture using a metal spoon or the plastic scraper (**H**).

13 Sprinkle some extra dark rye flour on the surface for decoration (**I**).

14 Allow the dough to rise for 1–2 hours, covered with the large mixing bowl or a shower cap. If your kitchen is fairly warm, you can just leave the loaf pan (covered with the shower cap or mixing bowl) on your work surface.

If your kitchen isn't that warm, **you'll need to follow the instructions on page 28**, but leave the covered loaf pan in the oven for **1–2 hours** rather than 30 minutes. Check the loaf every 30 minutes to see how it's doing.

You'll know that the loaf is ready to bake when it rises just over the pan and little cracks and air holes appear on the surface (J).

15 Set the oven temperature to 250°C (480°F) Gas 9 and place a deep roasting tray on the bottom surface.

16 When the loaf is ready to bake, remove the bowl or the shower cap that has been covering it and place the loaf pan in the preheated oven.

17 Pour a cup of water into the hot tray to form steam (**ask an adult to help with this**) and then lower the oven temperature to 220°C (425°F) Gas 7.

18 Bake the loaf for around 30 minutes until it is golden brown. Carefully turn the loaf out of the loaf pan. To check if it is baked through, tap the bottom of the loaf with your knuckles – it should sound hollow. Make sure the bread has cooled down before slicing it (**ask an adult to help with this**).

J

Puffy Pitta Pockets

The best part of this recipe is the moment that the pitta suddenly pops in the oven. They say that a watched pot never boils, but a watched pitta definitely pops! Just be careful when you take them out, as they get really hot. These pitta pockets are perfect stuffed with cherry tomatoes and Cheddar cheese.

Ingredients:

100 g/¾ cup plain/all-purpose flour, plus extra for dusting

100 g/¾ cup wholemeal/whole-wheat flour

4 g/1 teaspoon salt

2 g fresh/1 g/¼ teaspoon dried/active dry yeast

130 g/130 ml/½ cup water, cold

Equipment:

2 small mixing bowls

wooden spoon

large mixing bowl

plastic scraper

shower cap (optional)

baking tray or baking stone

rolling pin

deep roasting tray

wooden peel

resealable plastic bag

Makes 6 mini pitta breads

1 In a small mixing bowl, mix the flour and salt together and set aside with a wooden spoon. **This is the dry mixture**.

2 Weigh out the yeast and add it to the large mixing bowl. Add ¾ of the water to activate or dissolve the yeast (depending on which type of yeast you're using – **see page 22**). **This is the wet mixture.**

3 Mix the dry mixture into the wet mixture.

4 Stir the mixture slowly with your hands until it comes together. If it doesn't come together and it seems a bit dry, add a little of the remaining water. At this point the dough should be slightly sticky.

5 Use the plastic scraper to scape the sides of the bowl clean.

6 Cover the dough with the shower cap or small mixing bowl that contained the flour and leave to stand for 10 minutes.

7 Knead the dough, by following steps 1–9 on page 24.

8 Gently punch down the dough to release the trapped air.

9 Transfer the dough to a lightly floured wooden board or work surface. Divide the dough into 6 equal-sized portions with a plastic scraper (**A**). Shape the portions into balls.

10 Cover with the large mixing bowl and leave to rest for 10 minutes (**B**).

11 Preheat your oven to 250°C (480°F) Gas 9 and place a **baking tray** or a **baking stone** on the middle shelf.

12 Sprinkle a little more flour on the wooden board or work surface to help you roll and to stop the dough from sticking.

13 Remove the large mixing bowl covering the dough and and use a rolling pin to roll each piece of dough into a round or disc-shaped pitta until the dough starts to shrink slightly (**C**). When the dough shrinks, move on to the second piece and then the third etc.

14 Cover each disc after you've rolled it out to prevent a skin from forming.

15 After you have rolled out all 6 pieces, go back to the first. The dough should have relaxed making it easier to roll into the desired shape. Repeat the process until you are happy with all 6 of them, remembering to rest the dough if it starts to shrink. The pittas should be rolled to a thickness of about 3 mm/⅛ in. (**D**).

16 Leave to rise, covered with the large bowl for another 10 minutes.

17 Place the pittas on the preheated baking tray or baking stone using a wooden peel (**ask an adult to help**). After around 5 minutes, the pittas will suddenly puff up. When they do, they're ready!

18 Allow them to cool on a wire rack and either eat immediately (**be very careful, though, as the inside stays very hot for a while!**) or place them in a resealable plastic bag so they don't dry out.

B

D

Flowerpot Garlic Bread

These little garlic breads look fantastic baked in their sweet little flower pots. It's also really good fun to see them growing before your eyes in the oven. If you don't like garlic, you can leave it out, as the little breads will still taste great flavoured with rosemary. You can also bake the garlic bread as 2 separate loaves if you'd prefer to do it that way.

Ingredients:

600 g/4⅔ cups white strong/bread flour plus extra for dusting

10 g/1½ tablespoons chopped fresh rosemary or 3 g/1½ teaspoons dried oregano

12 g/1 tablespoon salt

400 g/400 ml/1⅔ cups water, warm

12 g fresh or 6 g/1½ tablespoons dried/active dried yeast

80 g/3 heads fresh garlic, finely sliced

soft butter, for greasing the pots/pan

semolina or polenta, for coating the flower pots

olive oil, for painting the surface

few sprigs of rosemary, for decoration

Equipment:

2 small mixing bowls

measuring jug/pitcher

plastic scraper

large mixing bowl

6 small flowerpots or 2 x 500-g/6 x 4-in. loaf pans

pastry brush for greasing the pots/pans

baking tray

deep roasting tray

Makes 6 small flowerpots or 2 loaves

1 In one of the small mixing bowls, add the flour, herbs and salt (**A**).

2 Mix everything together thoroughly with your fingers and set aside. **This is the dry mixture (B)**.

3 Weigh out the warm water in the measuring jug/pitcher and transfer ¾ of it into your large mixing bowl.

4 Weigh out the yeast and add it to the second small mixing bowl. Then add it to the water. If you're using dried/active dry yeast, you'll need to soak it for around 10 minutes or until it floats to the top and starts to bubble slightly. If you're using fresh yeast, dissolve it in warm water with your hands. If you're using instant/quick dry yeast or fast-acting yeast, see page 17. **This is the wet mixture**.

5 Add the dry mixture to the wet mixture and stir it slowly with your hands until it comes together (**C**). If it doesn't come together and it seems a bit dry, add a little of the remaining water. At this point the dough be slightly sticky.

6 Use the plastic scraper to scape the sides of the bowl clean.

7 Cover the mixture with a shower cap or the small bowl that originally contained the flour mixture and leave it to stand for 10 minutes (**D**).

8 Squash the dough with your knuckles and fingers to flatten out the lumps. It should now look pancake-shaped (**E**).

9 **Knead the dough, by following steps 1–9 on page 24 (F) (G) (H) (I).**

10 The dough will have increased in volume, so you'll need to gently punch down the dough again to release the trapped air.

11 Transfer the dough to a lightly floured wooden board or work surface using a plastic scraper (**J**).

12 If you want to bake the garlic bread in individual flowerpots, divide the dough into 6 equal portions using the scraper (**K**); if you'd prefer to bake the garlic bread as 2 separate loaves, divide the dough into 2 even portions.

L   M   N   O

13 Flatten each dough portion into a rectangular shape (**L**).

14 Place the thin slices of fresh garlic onto the flattened rectangular dough (**M**). It is up to you how garlicky you want your bread, so feel free to add more if you like.

15 Fold the sides of the dough into the middle (**N**).

16 Roll up the dough into a loaf shape (**O**).

17 Use a pastry brush to grease the inside of the flowerpots with butter and sprinkle a little semolina or polenta inside (**P**).

18 Place the portions of dough into each of the flowerpots (**Q**). Paint the top of the dough with the olive oil and stick a small sprig of rosemary in each one. If you're making loaves, place the portions of dough into the greased loaf pans and stick a sprig of rosemary into the top.

19 Put the flowerpots on a baking tray, as this will make them easier to load into the oven. Cover the flowerpots or loaf pans with clean mixing bowls and leave in a warm place (**see steps 3–4 on page 28**) for around 1 hour until the dough has risen over the top of the pots/pans.

P   Q

If your kitchen isn't that warm, follow the instructions on **page 28**, but leave the pots in the oven for **1 hour**, rather than 30 minutes.

20 Check how the dough is rising every 15 minutes. When it's risen to about **2–3 cm/¾–1 in.** above the surface of each pot, it's ready (**R**).

21 Preheat the oven to 250°C (480°F) Gas 9 and place a deep roasting tray on the bottom surface. Remember to remove the baking tray containing the flowerpots from the oven if you left it in there to let the dough rise!

22 Place the baking tray of flowerpots or the pans in the oven and pour a cup of water to the hot roasting tray to form steam (**ask an adult to help with this**). Then lower the oven temperature to 200°C (400°F) Gas 6.

23 Bake for around 20–35 minutes until the garlic breads have turned golden brown on top. Carefully turn the breads out of their flowerpots or loaf pans and allow to cool on a wire rack before tucking in!

"I really enjoyed kneading the dough for this recipe. I also loved the fact that the bread was baked in flowerpots!"
Sami (Aged 10)

The Perfect Sausage Roll

Familiar to many people in the UK, a hot, hearty sausage roll always brings a smile to people's faces! You can use almost any type of sausage to make them. Remember that the dough needs to rise in the refrigerator (preferably overnight), because the mixture contains meat.

Ingredients:

4 g fresh or 2 g/½ teaspoon dried/active dry yeast

20 g/4 teaspoons water, warm

4 g/1 teaspoon salt

200 g/1⅔ cups white strong/bread flour

2 medium eggs

30 g/2 tablespoons soft butter (salted or unsalted)

4 medium sausages or 400 g/14 oz. sausage meat, if preferred.

1 egg mixed with salt, to make the egg wash

Equipment:

large mixing bowl

2 small mixing bowls

fork, to beat the eggs

Danish whisk

plastic scraper

shower cap (optional)

rolling pin

disposable piping bag (optional)

pastry brush

baking tray lined with parchment paper

clingfilm/plastic wrap

deep roasting tray

Makes 4 large sausage rolls

1 In the large mixing bowl, dissolve or activate the yeast in the warm water depending on what type of yeast you're using (**see page 22**, unless you're using instant/quick dry yeast or fast-acting yeast, in which case, **see page 17**) (**A**). This is the **wet mixture**.

2 In a small mixing bowl mix the salt and the flour together and set aside. **This is the dry mixture**.

3 Crack the eggs into another small bowl, and lightly beat them with a fork.

4 Add the beaten egg to the wet mixture, then add the dry mixture on top (**B**).

5 Mix with a Danish whisk (if you have one) or a wooden spoon until it all comes together as a rough, sticky dough.

6 Scrape the sides of the bowl clean using a plastic scraper (**C**).

7 Spoon the butter onto the top of the dough (**D**).

8 Cover the dough with a shower cap or the small mixing bowl that contained the dry mixture. Leave it to stand for 10 minutes.

9 Start to incorporate the butter. Pull a portion of the dough up from the side and press it into the middle (**E**). Turn the bowl 90° clockwise and pull another portion of the dough up from the side and press it into the middle. Repeat this process another **8 times.** The whole process should only take 10–20 seconds.

10 Turn the ball of dough over in the bowl and make a finger mark in it to indicate that you've kneaded it once.

11 Cover the dough again with a shower cap or the small mixing bowl. Leave the mixture to rest for 10 minutes.

12 Repeat steps 9, 10 and 11 another 3 times (so you will have kneaded the dough **4 times**) (**F**).

13 Place the dough in the fridge for at least 1 hour, but ideally overnight, covered with an upturned small bowl or shower cap.

14 The dough will now be cold and easy to work with. Lightly flour a work surface. Use a rolling pin to roll out the dough into a rectangle around 3 mm/⅛ in. thick, 20 cm/8 in. wide and 30 cm/12 in. long (**G**, over the page).

15 If you are using sausages, you'll need 4 in total. Remove the filling from the casings and place 2 of them along the top of the dough you have rolled out. Make sure that this meat filling extends end-to-end across the dough. If you're using sausage meat instead of sausages, fill a disposable piping bag and pipe the meat into a long strip across along the top of the dough.

16 Fold the dough over the sausage meat and brush egg wash directly below the meat strip (**H**, over the page). Roll the dough over, making sure that the top part sticks to the egg wash.

17 Use a knife to cut the roll away from the remaining pastry (**ask an adult to help**). Repeat the process with the remaining dough to create another sausage roll (**I**, over the page).

18 Cut the sausage rolls in two to create 4 of them. Place them on the prepared baking tray and cover lightly with clingfilm/plastic wrap and place in the refrigerator.

19 Allow to rise until the sausage rolls have nearly doubled in volume. When they are ready, preheat the oven to 200°C (400°F) Gas 6 and place a deep roasting tray on the base.

20 Remove the clingfilm/plastic wrap, then brush some of the remaining egg wash onto the sausage rolls.

21 Make 7–8 diagonal marks on the surface of each sausage roll using a knife (**ask an adult to help with this**) for decoration (**J**, over the page).

22 Place the sausage rolls in the preheated oven and pour a cup of water into the roasting tray (**ask an adult to help**).

23 Bake for around 30 minutes until golden brown. Carefully transfer the sausage rolls to a wire rack to cool before eating, because the inside will be very hot!

E

F

G

H

I

J

Crunchy Breadsticks

These crunchy, more-ish snacks are great both on their own or dunked into dips. They make a good starter, too, particularly before a pizza, which you'll learn how to make next. See how steady you can keep your hand while piping the mixture into sticks!

A

Ingredients:

50 g/3½ tablespoons water

25 g/1½ tablespoons olive oil

40 g/⅓ cup white strong/bread flour

4 g/1 teaspoon salt

25 g/¼ cup sesame seeds

1 egg

Equipment:

measuring jug/pitcher

small mixing bowl

saucepan

wooden spoon

piping bag

baking sheet lined with parchment paper

Makes about 16

1 Add the water and the olive oil to the measuring jug/pitcher.

2 Place the flour and salt in the small mixing bowl and set aside.

3 Heat up a saucepan over a medium heat (**ask an adult to help with this**) and add the sesame seeds, stirring them with a wooden spoon to stop them from burning. Cook them until they turn golden.

4 Add the olive oil mixture and the flour mixture to the saucepan and cook until it all comes together into a ball (**A**). Be careful that it doesn;t burn!

5 Take the saucepan off the heat and transfer the cooked mixture into the bowl that contained the flour. Leave the mixture to cool slightly.

6 While the mixture cools, break the egg into the jug/pitcher and beat it lightly with a fork.

7 Once the mixture is warm add the lightly beaten egg little by little until it is completely incorporated and the mixture is nice and smooth (**B**).

8 Fill a piping bag with the mixture, cut a 5 mm/⅛ in. tip at the end (**ask an adult to help with this**) and pipe the mixture into long sticks on the prepared baking tray (**C**).

9 Preheat your oven to 250°C (480°F) Gas 9 and place a deep roasting tray on the base of the oven.

10 Place the tray with the sesame sticks in the preheated oven and pour a cup of water into the hot tray to form steam (**ask an adult to help with this**), then lower the oven temperature to 200°C 400°F Gas 6.

11 Bake for 10–15 minutes until golden brown. Allow the breadsticks to cool on a wire rack before dunking into dips and munching!

"I loved squeezing the dough out of the squeezy piping tube onto the tray to make the breadsticks. My breadsticks were delicious!"
Ayse (Aged 8)

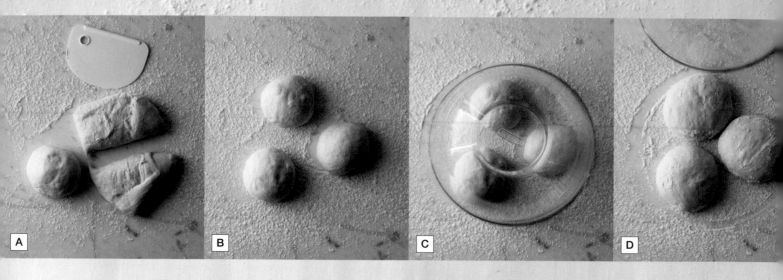

A

B

C

D

Pizza Dough

Pizza tastes so much better when you've baked it yourself. It also means you can be as generous with the toppings as you like! You'll find a recipe for a classic Margherita Pizza on pages 98–99, but you can also try something a little different by substituting tomato and mozzarella for apple, blueberries, cranberries and flavoured sugar for a sensational Sweet Pizza (see pages 100–101). Bear in mind that you'll need to prepare the dough the day before you make either of these recipes.

Ingredients:

300 g/2¼ cups white strong/bread flour

6 g/1½ teaspoons salt

1 g fresh or 0.5 g/⅛ teaspoon dried/active dry yeast

180 g/180 ml/¾ cup water

Equipment:

small mixing bowl

large mixing bowl

plastic scraper

shower cap

rolling pin

baking tray lined with parchment paper

deep roasting tray

Makes 3 pizzas

1 In the small mixing bowl, mix the flour and salt together and set aside. **This is the dry mixture.**

2 In the large mixing bowl, weigh out the yeast. Add ¾ of the water to activate or dissolve the yeast (**see page 22**, unless you're using instant/quick dry yeast or fast-acting yeast, in which case, **see page 17**). **This is the wet mixture.**

3 Once the yeast has dissolved, add the dry mixture and mix slowly with your hands until it comes together. If it doesn't come together and it seems a bit dry, add a little of the remaining water and mix until it forms a rough dough. At this point the dough should be slightly sticky.

4 Use a plastic scraper to scrape the sides of the bowl clean and make sure all the ingredients are thoroughly mixed together.

5 Cover the mixture with a shower cap or with the small mixing bowl and let it stand for 10 minutes.

6 After 10 minutes, lift a portion of the dough up from the side and fold it into the middle. Turn the bowl 90° and repeat this process with another portion of dough. Repeat until you've lifted and folded the dough 10 times.

7 Turn the ball of dough over in the bowl. Wet your finger and make a finger mark in it to indicate that you've kneaded it once.

8 Cover with the shower cap or with the bowl that contained the flour. Leave the mixture to rest for 10 minutes.

9 Repeat the entire lifting and folding process another 3 times (so you've lifted and folded the dough a total of 40 times), making sure the mixture is covered between kneads and remembering to mark the dough to indicate the number of kneads you've done.

F

10 Cover the dough and leave it to rise for **16–24 hours** or until the dough has almost doubled in volume.

11 The next day, gently punch down the dough to release the trapped air.

12 On a lightly floured work surface, cut the dough into 3 even portions using a plastic scraper (**A**).

13 Roll the 3 dough portions into balls using your hands (**B**).

14 Cover them with the large bowl (**C**) to prevent a skin from forming and leave to rest for 15 minutes. Leave a little gap between the dough balls to allow them to expand

15 By this time, the dough will have almost doubled in volume (**D**).

16 Use a rolling pin to roll out each ball of dough into a disc (**E**) until the dough starts to shrink.

17 Add a light sprinkling of flour (**F**) to help you roll and to stop the dough from sticking. When this happens, move on to the second piece and then the third. Cover each disc after you've rolled it out to prevent a skin from forming.

18 After you have rolled out the third piece go back to the first. The dough should have relaxed making it easier to roll into the desired shape. Repeat the process until you are happy with all three, remembering to rest the dough if it starts to shrink. Your dough is now ready! Make sure you cover the discs to prevent a skin from forming.

There is another way of preparing the dough, which will require a little more practice, but it's how the professionals do it, so it'd be great to show off to your friends:

12A On a lightly floured work surface, shape the dough into 3 even portions using a plastic scraper, then roll the portions into balls. Cover them with the large mixing bowl to prevent a skin from forming and leave to rest for 15 minutes.

13A Sprinkle a little flour on your hands and on the first dough ball to stop it from sticking and gently press the dough into a disc. Cover it and move on to the second and third dough balls, making sure to cover them when you're not shaping them.

14A Carefully drape the first disc over your closed fists.

15A With your thumbs down move you hands up and down tugging and stretching the dough evenly with your knuckles, making sure you are focusing on the edges of the dough, not in the middle. Do this in a circular motion.

16A The middle will stretch on its own. If you go too close to the middle it will get too thin and possibly break, but don't worry you can always patch it up if this happens.

17A Now extend your thumbs and stretch the dough between them while moving in a circular pattern to give the edges a final thinning. Be careful not to apply too much pressure, as you might go through the dough. If you are feeling adventurous, you can toss the pizza in the air, but make sure you catch it!

You can now start adding toppings to your pizza (**see pages 98–101**)!

Margherita Pizza

Ingredients:

1 disc of dough (see page 96)

handful of semolina

tomato passata/strained tomatoes

1 large mozzarella ball

6–8 fresh basil leaves

olive oil

course salt

Equipment:

baking tray or pizza stone

parchment paper

pizza peel or paddle

large serving spoon

Makes 1 pizza

1 Preheat your oven to 250°C (480°F) Gas 9. Put a heavy baking tray turned upside-down and lined with parchment paper or a pizza stone on the middle shelf of the oven. I prefer to use a tray as I find it heats up much quicker.

2 Lightly sprinkle some semolina on the pizza peel or paddle and place the dough disc on top of the semolina. The semolina stops the dough from sticking and will help when you come to slide the pizza onto the baking tray or pizza stone. Alternatively, place the dough disc on parchment paper.

3 Spoon the tomato passata/strained tomatoes onto the dough leaving a 2 cm/¾ in. edge. Tear a few chunks of mozzarella and place them, fairly evenly spaced, on top.

4 Scatter a few basil leaves. Finally, drizzle with a little olive oil and sprinkle a little salt on top.

5 Slide the pizza onto the upside-down hot tray or baking stone in the oven with the peel. Alternatively, remove the hot baking tray with oven mitts and place it on a wire cooling rack. Use the oven mitts to pick up the parchment paper with the pizza on top and carefully place it on the hot baking tray.

6 Place the hot tray back in the oven (**ask an adult to help with this**). Bake for 3–7 minutes according to how crispy you like your pizza. Allow to cool slightly on a wire rack, cut into slices and enjoy as soon as possible!

Sweet Pizza

Ingredients:

1 disc of dough (see page 96)

handful of semolina

2 large apples, finely sliced

handful of blueberries

handful of cranberries

1 tablespoon cinnamon sugar

Equipment:

baking tray or pizza stone

parchment paper

pizza peel or paddle

Makes 1 pizza

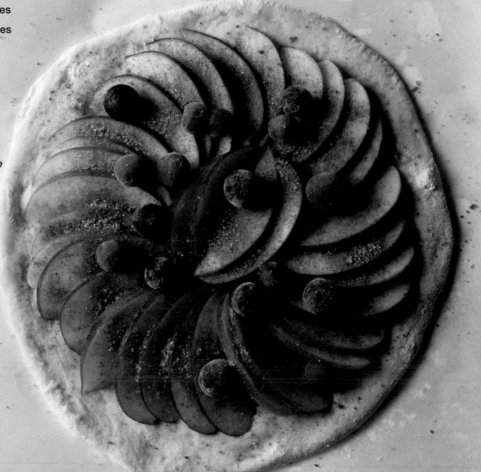

1 Preheat your oven to 250°C (480°F) Gas 9. Put a heavy baking tray turned upside-down and lined with parchment paper or a pizza stone on the middle shelf of the oven.

2 Lightly sprinkle some semolina on the pizza peel or paddle and place the dough disc on top of the semolina. The semolina stops the dough from sticking and will help when you

come to slide the pizza onto the baking tray or pizza stone. Alternatively, place the dough disc on parchment paper.

3 Cut up the apples and arrange the slices neatly in a circle on the dough, leaving enough to cover the central hole and leaving a 2 cm/¾ in. edge around the outside. Scatter a few berries, then sprinkle the cinnamon sugar on top.

4 Slide the pizza onto the upside-down hot tray or baking stone in the oven with the peel. Alternatively, remove the hot baking tray with oven mitts and place it on a wire cooling rack. Use the oven mitts to pick up the parchment paper with the pizza on top and carefully place it on the hot baking tray.

5 Then place the hot tray back in the oven (**ask an adult to help with this**). Bake for 3–7 minutes according to how crispy you like your pizza. Allow to cool slightly on a wire rack, cut into slices and enjoy as soon as possible!

Minestrone Sourdough

Ingredients:

300 g/2¼ cups white strong/bread flour, plus extra for dusting

5 g/1 teaspoon celery salt

3 g/½ teaspoon salt

20 g/¼ cup coarsely grated fresh potato

30 g/¼ cup coarsely grated fresh celeriac/celery root

30 g/¼ cup coarsely grated fresh carrot

30 g/¼ cup finely chopped fresh leek

10 g/2 teaspoons finely sliced red onion

2 g/½ teaspoon dried oregano

40 g/1½ oz. tomato purée/paste

180 g/180 ml/¾ cup water, warm

200 g/ 1 cup white sourdough starter (see pages 36–38)

15 g/1 tablespoon olive oil

Equipment:

2 large mixing bowls

2 small mixing bowls

cheese grater

shower cap

4 proofing baskets (800-g/1¾-lbs. capacity) or colander, floured

deep roasting tray

small peel, floured

pastry brush

Makes 4 small loaves

This filling bread is infused with an array of flavours – potato, celeriac/celery root, carrot, leek, red onion, garlic and oregano – all the components of a hearty minestrone soup. It's fantastic for a winter's day and feels like a meal in itself! Because this recipe involves a sourdough starter, it will take some time to make, but it'll be worth it!

1 In a small mixing bowl, mix the flour and the two types of salt together thoroughly and set aside. **This is the dry mixture.**

2 In a separate small mixing bowl, add the grated potato, grated celeriac/celery root, grated carrot, chopped leek (just the green part), sliced red onion and the dried oregano and make sure all the ingredients are thoroughly mixed together.

3 In one of the large mixing bowls, dissolve the tomato purée/paste in the water, add the sourdough starter and mix until dissolved (if the sourdough is stiff, break it into little pieces). This is the **wet mixture.**

4 Put the olive oil in the other large mixing bowl and set aside.

5 Mix the dry mixture with the vegetable mixture.

6 Add the wet mixture to the combined dry mixture and vegetable mixture and mix until it comes together and forms a rough dough.

7 Coat the sides of the bowl containing the olive oil with the oil, take the rough dough and place it in the bowl. Cover this bowl with a shower cap or with the bowl that contained the dry mixture and leave to stand for 10 minutes.

8 Knead the dough for 10 seconds (**see page 24 for the technique**), or until the dough resists. Leave to stand for 10 minutes.

9 Knead the dough another 3 times, covering the bowl with a shower cap or with the small mixing bowl between kneading and leaving it to stand for 10 minutes between each time.

10 After the final time, cover and allow the dough to rest for 1 hour. Flour the proofing baskets.

11 Remove the dough from the large bowl, lightly sprinkle it with flour and divide it into 4 portions, shaped into balls. Place the balls of dough into the floured proofing baskets (**A**).

12 Allow the dough to proof (rise) until it has doubled in size, which should take between 3 and 6 hours. If your kitchen is fairly warm, you can just leave the proofing baskets on your work surface.

If your kitchen isn't that warm, **you'll need to follow the instructions on page 28**, but leave the proofing baskets in the turned-off oven for **3–6 hours** rather than 30 minutes.

13 When it has risen, place the loaves in the refrigerator for 30 minutes. Meanwhile, preheat the oven to 250°C (480°F) Gas 9 and place a deep roasting tray on the bottom surface of the oven.

14 Remove the loaves from the refrigerator, carefully remove it from the proofing basket and place it on the lightly floured peel (**B**).

15 Place the loaves in the preheated oven and pour a cup of water onto the hot tray to create steam (**ask an adult to help with this**). Lower the oven temperature to 220°C (425°F) Gas 7.

16 Bake the loaves for about 35 minutes until golden brown. You'll know when they're baked properly when you get a hollow sound when tapping it on the bottom with your knuckles. Allow the bread to cool on a wire rack before serving.

teatime
with friends

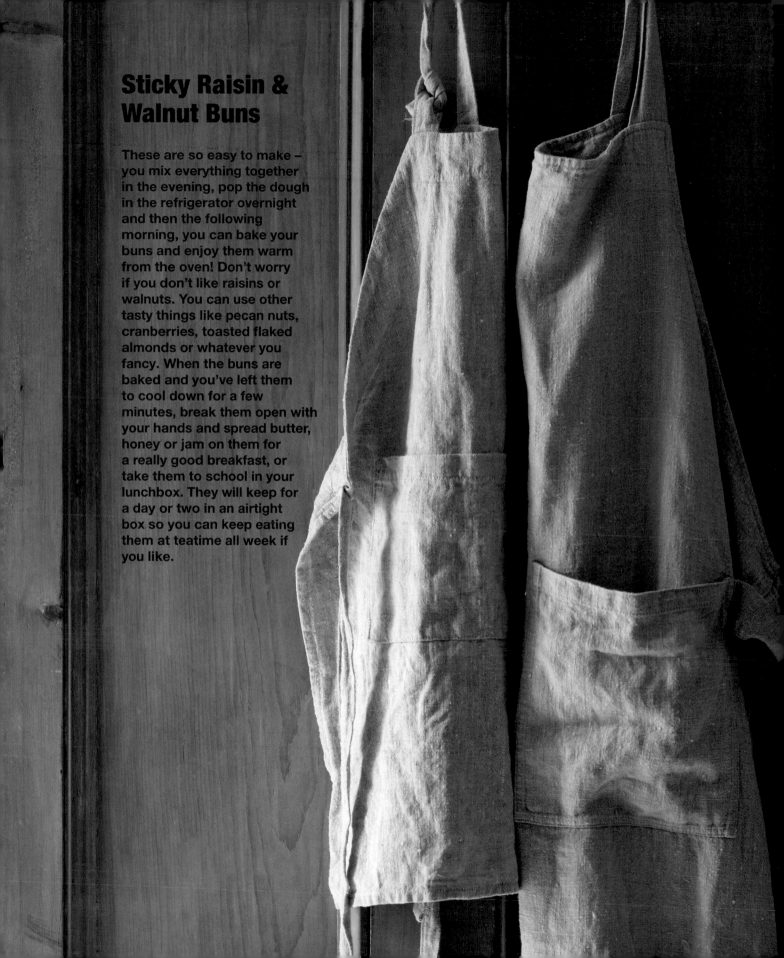

Sticky Raisin & Walnut Buns

These are so easy to make –
you mix everything together
in the evening, pop the dough
in the refrigerator overnight
and then the following
morning, you can bake your
buns and enjoy them warm
from the oven! Don't worry
if you don't like raisins or
walnuts. You can use other
tasty things like pecan nuts,
cranberries, toasted flaked
almonds or whatever you
fancy. When the buns are
baked and you've left them
to cool down for a few
minutes, break them open with
your hands and spread butter,
honey or jam on them for
a really good breakfast, or
take them to school in your
lunchbox. They will keep for
a day or two in an airtight
box so you can keep eating
them at teatime all week if
you like.

B

C

D

Ingredients:

75 g/½ cup wholemeal/ whole-wheat flour

100 g/¾ cup white strong/bread flour

4 g/¾ teaspoon salt

50 g/⅓ cup raisins

50 g/⅓ cup walnuts, chopped into small pieces

1 teaspoon freshly grated orange zest

4 g fresh yeast or 2 g/½ teaspoon dried/active dry yeast

200 g/200 ml/¾ cup water, warm

Makes about 12

Equipment:

2 large mixing bowls

small mixing bowl

measuring jug/pitcher

Danish whisk (optional)

wooden spoon

plastic scraper

shower cap

deep roasting tray

pastry brush

bun/cupcake pan, greased with vegetable oil

1 In one of the large mixing bowls, mix together the wholemeal/whole-wheat flour, strong/bread flour and salt with your hands or a large spoon. Make sure everything is thoroughly mixed together and set aside. **This is the dry mixture.**

2 In a small mixing bowl, mix together the raisins, chopped walnuts and orange zest with your hands or a large spoon and set aside. **This is the fruit mixture.**

3 Weigh out the water in the measuring jug/pitcher and transfer ¾ of it into another large mixing bowl.

4 Weigh out the yeast and add it to the water. If you're using dried/active dry yeast, soak it for 10 minutes or until it floats to the top and starts to bubble. If you're using fresh yeast, dissolve it in warm water with your hands. If you're using instant/quick dry yeast or fast-acting yeast, **see page 17. This is the wet mixture.**

5 Now, add the fruit mixture to the dry mixture (A) and mix thoroughly with a Danish whisk or a wooden spoon **(B)**.

6 Add the combined fruit mixture and dry mixture to the large mixing bowl containing the wet mixture **(C)**.

7 Mix with the Danish whisk or wooden spoon until you can't see any more dry blobs of flour. **The mixture should have a sticky consistency.** If it doesn't, you may need to add a little of the remaining water.

8 Use a plastic scraper to scrape the inside of the bowl to loosen any sticky bits of dough. Then gently push the loose bits into the mixture so that the sides of your bowl are now nice and clean.

9 Cover the bowl. You can either use a shower cap or place an even larger bowl upside-down over it **(D)**. Now put the mixture in the refrigerator overnight!

Note: If you're using dried/active dry yeast, instant/quick dry yeast or fast-acting yeast, it's best to leave the mixture on your work surface for 30 minutes before putting it in the refrigerator overnight.

E

F

10 The next day, take the dough out of the refrigerator and take the shower cap or bowl off it The mixture will be bubbly (**E**).

11 Preheat your oven to 250°C (480°F) Gas 9 and put a deep roasting tray in the bottom of the oven.

12 Using a pastry brush, lightly grease the bun/cupcake pan – especially the holes – with some vegetable oil.

13 Fill a clean small bowl with water. Dip a tablespoon into the water to wet it.

14 Take a scoopful of dough with the tablespoon and place it in one of the holes in the greased pan so that it fills up ¾ of the hole. Keep taking tablespoonfuls of the dough and dropping each blob into a hole in the pan (**F**). You can wet the tablespoon in the bowl of water again if you need to.

15 If you have filled all the holes in the bun/cupcake pan, cover the bowl of dough again and keep it for later.

16 Ask an adult to help you put the bun pan in the preheated oven and pour a cup of water into the hot roasting tray in the bottom of the oven: this will form steam and help the buns to form a lovely crust.

17 Lower the oven temperature to 200°C (400°F) Gas 6.

18 Bake the buns for 15–20 minutes until they're golden brown. If you want to check whether they're properly baked, **ask an adult to help you** lift a bun out of the pan with oven mitts and tap the bottom with your knuckles. If it sounds hollow, the buns are ready.

19 Using oven mitts, carefully turn the other buns out of the pan and allow them to cool on a wire rack.

Potato and Onion Buns

These buns are fantastic for sandwiches or just as a tasty savoury snack to nibble on, but beware – they really are quite addictive! The dill really complements the potato and onion and these three ingredients go nicely with a smoked salmon and cream cheese filling. Like the previous recipe, they take 2 days to make.

Ingredients:

75 g/½ cup plus 1 tablespoon wholemeal/whole-wheat flour

100 g/¾ cup white strong/bread flour

170 g/170 ml/¾ cup water, warm

4 g fresh yeast or 2 g/½ teaspoon dried/active dry yeast

2 g/1 teaspoon dill seed

5 g/1¼ teaspoons salt

50 g/1 medium potato, peeled and finely grated

25 g/3 tablespoons red onion, finely chopped

Equipment:

2 small mixing bowls

measuring jug/pitcher

large mixing bowl

wooden spoon

Danish whisk (optional)

plastic scraper

shower cap (optional)

very large mixing bowl (optional)

deep roasting tray

baking tray lined with parchment paper

Makes about 12

1 In one of the small mixing bowls, mix together the wholemeal/whole-wheat flour and strong/bread flour with your hands or a large spoon. Make sure everything is thoroughly mixed together and set aside. **This is the dry mixture**.

2 Weigh out the water in the measuring jug/pitcher and transfer ¾ of it into your large mixing bowl.

3 Weigh out the yeast and add it to the water in the large mixing bowl. If you're using dried/active dry yeast, soak it for 10 minutes or until it floats to the top and starts to bubble. If you're using fresh yeast, dissolve it in warm water with your hands. If you're using instant/quick dry yeast or fast-acting yeast, **see page 17**. **This is the wet mixture**.

4 In the other small mixing bowl, mix together the dill seed, salt, finely grated potato and finely chopped red onion with your hands or a wooden spoon and set aside. **This is the vegetable mixture**.

5 Once the wet mixture is ready, add the dry mixture and the vegetable mixture to it.

6 Mix thoroughly with a wooden spoon or a Danish whisk until you can't see any more dry blobs of flour. **The mixture should have a sticky consistency**. If it doesn't, you may need to add a little of the remaining water.

7 Use a plastic scraper to scrape the insides of the bowl to loosen any sticky bits of dough. Gently push the loose bits into the mixture so that the sides of your bowl are now nice and clean.

8 Cover the bowl with either a shower cap or an even larger bowl placed upside-down over it.

Note: If you're using dried/active dry yeast, instant/quick dry yeast or fast-acting yeast, leave the mixture on your work surface for 30 minutes before putting it in the refrigerator overnight.

9 **The next day**, take the dough out of the refrigerator and remove the shower cap or bowl.

10 Preheat your oven to 250°C (480°F) Gas 9 and place a deep roasting tray on the base of the oven.

11 Place the prepared baking tray on your work surface. Take a scoopful of dough with the tablespoon and place it on baking tray in a round or oval-shape, leaving enough space between each bun so that they don't stick together.

12 **Ask an adult to help you** put the prepared baking tray in the preheated oven and pour a cup of water into the hot roasting tray in the bottom of the oven: this will form steam in the oven and help the buns to form a lovely crust.

13 Lower the oven temperature to 200°C (400°F) Gas 6.

14 Bake the buns for 15–20 minutes until they're golden brown. If you want to check whether they're properly baked, **ask an adult to help you** lift a bun out of the tray with oven mitts and tap the bottom with your knuckles. If it sounds hollow, the buns are ready.

15 Using oven mitts, carefully lift the other buns off the tray and allow them to cool on a wire rack. Enjoy with your choice of filling!

Sticky Apple and Cinnamon Buns

These buns are really sticky and moist because they're packed with lots of tangy apple. Don't bake them in muffin cases because they'll stick to them! Use the same bun/cupcake pan as the raisin and walnut buns, or you can create your own shapes. Remember that this recipe also takes 2 days to make.

Ingredients:

100 g/1 medium Granny Smith or cooking apple, cored with skin still on and cut into small pieces

30 g/2½ tablespoons caster/granulated sugar, plus extra for decoration

grated zest of ½ an unwaxed lemon

4 g/¾ teaspoon ground cinnamon

50 g/50 ml/¼ cup water

75 g/½ cup wholemeal/whole-wheat flour

100 g/¾ cup white stong/bread flour

3 g/¾ teaspoon salt

50 g/½ cup dried apple, cut into small pieces

4 g/¾ teaspoon fresh yeast or 2 g/½ teaspoon dried/active dry yeast

100 g/100 ml/⅓ cup water, warm

extra apple slices, for decoration

Equipment:

small saucepan

3 small mixing bowls

measuring jug/pitcher

large mixing bowl

wooden spoon

plastic scraper

shower cap (optional)

very large mixing bowl (optional)

pastry brush for greasing the bun/cupcake pan

bun/cupcake pan, greased with soft butter

deep roasting tray

Makes 7–8 depending on pan size

1 In a small saucepan over a medium heat, cook the apple, sugar, lemon zest, ground cinnamon and the water, stirring from time to time so it does not burn. Once the apple is soft take the pan off the heat and set aside to cool. **This is the softened apple mixture.**

2 In one of the small mixing bowls mix the wholemeal/whole-wheat flour, strong/bread flour, and salt together thoroughly and set aside. **This is the dry mixture.**

3 In another small mixing bowl, add the chopped dried apple and the softened apple mixture together and set aside.

4 Weigh out the water in the measuring jug/pitcher and transfer ¾ of it into your large mixing bowl.

5 Weigh out the yeast and add it to the water in the large mixing bowl. If you're using dried/active dry yeast, soak it for 10 minutes or until it floats to the top and bubbles. If you're using fresh yeast, dissolve it in warm water with your hands. If you're using instant/quick dry yeast or fast-acting yeast, **see page 17. This is the wet mixture.**

6 Add the dry mixture and the warm apple mixture to the wet mixture and mix thoroughly with a wooden spoon. **The mixture should have a sticky consistency.** If it doesn't, you may need to add a little of the remaining water.

7 Using a plastic scraper, scrape down the sides of the bowl to make sure that none of the mixture is stuck to the side of the bowl.

8 Cover the bowl. You can either use a shower cap or place an even larger bowl upside-down over it. Put the mixture in the fridge overnight.

Note: If you're using dried/active dry yeast, it's best to leave the mixture on your work surface for 30 minutes before putting it in the refrigerator overnight.

9 **The next day**, take the dough out of the refrigerator and remove the shower cap or bowl.

10 Preheat your oven to 250°C (480°F) Gas 9 and place a roasting tray on the bottom surface.

11 Using a pastry brush, lightly grease the bun/cupcake pan – especially the holes – with soft butter and coat with a thin layer of flour so that the mixture does not stick.

12 Take the dough out of the refrigerator.

13 Dip a wet tablespoon into the dough, scoop up a spoonful and drop it into the holes in the greased pan. You may need to wet the tablespoon in-between scoops.

14 Add 3 slices of apple to the top of the dough and sprinkle with sugar.

15 Place the bun/cupcake pan in the preheated oven and pour a cup of water to the hot roasting tray (**ask an adult to help with this**).

16 Lower the oven temperature to 200°C (400°F) Gas 6.

17 Bake for around 15–25 minutes until golden brown. If you want to check whether the buns are properly baked, **ask an adult to help you** lift a bun out of the pan with oven mitts and tap the bottom with your knuckles. If it sounds hollow, the buns are ready!

18 Using oven mitts, carefully turn the other buns out of the tray and allow them to cool on a wire rack before serving.

Sweet Rice and Raisin Bread

This gluten-free treat is great for anyone who loves rice pudding, and I'm definitely one of those people. The dough mixture even smells like rice pudding while you're making it, which means that you look forward to eating it that little bit more. This bread is fantastic thickly sliced and then toasted. Why not enjoy it spread with butter alongside a nice cup of hot chocolate?

Ingredients:

25 g/2 tablespoons white long grain rice

125 g/125 ml/½ cup water (for the rice)

200 g/200 ml/¾ cup water, warm (for the yeast)

8 g fresh yeast or 4 g/1 teaspoon dried/active dry yeast

50 g/⅓ cup rice flour

100 g/¾ cup potato starch

50 g/⅓ cup buckwheat flour

80 g/½ cup sultanas/golden raisins

6 g/1 teaspoon ground cinnamon

2 g/½ teaspoon salt

5 g/1 teaspoon runny honey

Equipment:

small saucepan and lid

measuring jug/pitcher

large mixing bowl

small mixing bowl

wooden spoon

shower cap (optional)

pastry brush for greasing the tray

500-g/6 x 4-in loaf pan, greased with vegetable oil

deep roasting tray

Makes 1 loaf

1 **Prepare the rice** by adding it to a small saucepan and add the water.

2 Bring the rice to the boil, cover the saucepan and simmer for about 15 minutes.

3 Once the rice is cooked through, take the pan off the heat and allow to cool.

4 Weigh out the water in the measuring jug/pitcher and transfer ¾ of it into your large mixing bowl.

5 Weigh out the yeast and add it to the water in the large mixing bowl. If you're using dried/active dry yeast, soak it for 10 minutes or until it floats to the top and bubbles. If you're using fresh yeast, dissolve it in warm water with your hands. If you're using instant/quick dry yeast or fast-acting yeast, **see page 17**. **This is the wet mixture (A)**.

6 In a small mixing bowl weigh out the rice flour, potato starch, buckwheat flour, sultanas/golden raisins, ground cinnamon and salt and set aside. **This is the dry mixture**.

7 Add the cooled rice, the dry mixture and the honey to the wet mixture (**B**).

8 Mix thoroughly with a wooden spoon until the batter is a thick pouring yogurt consistency (**C**). If it isn't, add a little of the remaining water.

9 Cover the mixture with the bowl that contained the dry mixture or a shower cap and allow to rise for 1 hour (**D**).

10 After 1 hour stir the mixture with a wooden spoon to deflate the air bubbles (**E**).

11 Carefully pour and spoon the mixture into the prepared loaf pan (**F**).

12 Cover with a clean shower cap or the large bowl again.

13 Allow the mixture to rise in a warm place until it just reaches the top of the pan, which will take around 30 minutes. If your kitchen isn't that warm, follow the instructions on **page 28** and check to see how the loaf is rising after 15 minutes.

14 You will know when the mixture is ready for baking because cracks and little air holes will appear on the surface (**G**). The mixture will only rise about 2 cm/¾ in. as it doesn't contain gluten.

15 Set the oven to 250°C (480°F) Gas 9 and place a deep roasting tray at the bottom.

16 Place the loaf in the oven (once it's heated up) and pour a cup of water into the hot tray to form steam (**ask an adult to help with this**).

17 Lower the oven temperature to 220°C (425°F) Gas 7.

18 Bake for around 35 minutes until golden brown. Check that the loaf is baked by carefully turning it out of its pan and tapping the loaf on the bottom with your knuckles (**ask an adult to help with this**). If you hear a hollow sound, it's ready!

19 Allow to cool on a wire rack before you slice it and enjoy it! (**H**)

E

F

G

H

Gingerbread Family

Ingredients:

60 g/5 tablespoons dark brown sugar

50 g/3 tablespoons golden syrup/light corn syrup

1 egg

200 g/1½ cups white strong/bread flour, plus extra for dusting

12 g/2½ teaspoons ground ginger

4 g/1 teaspoon mixed spice/apple pie spice

1 g/small pinch of salt

20 g/1½ tablespoons butter

10 g fresh or 5 g/1¼ teaspoons dried/active dry yeast

20 g/20 ml/1 tablespoon milk, warm

Makes about 10, depending on size of cutters

Equipment:

2 small mixing bowls

microwave or small saucepan

2 large mixing bowls

measuring jug/pitcher

Danish whisk (optional)

plastic scraper

shower cap (optional)

rolling pin

ruler

set of gingerbread men cutters

2 baking trays, lined with parchment paper

deep roasting tray

chopstick or wooden skewer

If you like gingerbread men, you will love this family! They're quite similar to gingerbread biscuits/cookies but even tastier with a great ginger flavour. It's lots of fun creating their faces and even making clothes for them – try sticking on Smartie buttons or raisin shoes. If you make two lots of the dough, you could make a whole classroom and adapt each shape to look like your friends!

1 In a small mixing bowl, mix the sugar, golden syrup/light corn syrup and the egg thoroughly with a wooden spoon and set aside. **This is the wet mixture (A).**

2 In another small mixing bowl, mix the flour, ground ginger, mixed spice/apple pie spice and salt thoroughly with your hands or a wooden spoon and set aside. **This is the dry mixture.**

3 **Ask an adult to help you** melt the butter in a microwave or in a small saucepan on the stove. **Once it's just melted, pour it into a large mixing bowl and set aside.**

4 Add the milk to the large mixing bowl. Weigh out the yeast and then add it to the milk. If you're using dried/active dry yeast, soak it for 10 minutes or until it floats to the top and starts to bubble slightly. If you're using fresh yeast, dissolve it in the milk with your hands. If you're using instant/quick dry yeast or fast-acting yeast, **see page 17. This is the yeast mixture.**

5 Add the dry mixture and then the wet mixture to the yeast mixture (**B**).

6 Mix everything together thoroughly with a Danish whisk or a wooden spoon until you can't see any more dry blobs of flour (**C**).

7 Using a plastic scraper, scrape the insides of the bowl to loosen any sticky bits of dough. Gently push the loose bits into the mixture so that the sides of your bowl are now nice and clean.

8 Tip the mixture into the large bowl of melted butter (**D**).

9 Cover the bowl. You can either use a clean shower cap or place a clean large mixing bowl upside down over it (**E**). Allow the dough to rest for 10 minutes.

10 After 10 minutes, the dough is ready to be kneaded. Leaving it in the bowl, push the dough with your knuckles a few times to squash it (**F**).

11 Pull a portion of the dough up from the side and press it into the middle (**G**). Turn the bowl 90° clockwise and pull another portion of dough up from the side and press it into the middle. Repeat another 8–10 times and you will start to get a big smooth blob. The dough will be stiff.

12 Press one finger into the dough to indicate that you have kneaded it once.

13 Cover the bowl with the shower cap or bowl again and allow it to rest for 10 minutes.

14 Repeat **steps 11–13 another 3 times**, so you will have kneaded the dough a total of 4 times. You should now have 4 finger marks in the dough. (**H**) The mixture should be smooth. If it isn't, you'll have to knead it another 1–2 times.

15 Cover the bowl again and allow it to rise for 1 hour at room temperature. If the dough isn't covered, it will form a skin, which would affect the gingerbread later.

16 After 1 hour, uncover the bowl and gently punch down the dough with your fist to flatten it slightly.

I   J   K   L

17 Sprinkle a little bit of flour on a clean work surface. This will stop the dough from sticking to it.

18 Take the dough out of the bowl and put it on the lightly floured work surface. Sprinkle a little bit more flour on top of the dough – this will stop the rolling pin from sticking to your dough. Start to roll the rolling pin and keep rolling back and forth until you get an oval shape (**I**).

19 Use a ruler to measure the thickness of the dough. You want to stop rolling it when it is about 2–3 mm/¹⁄₁₆ in. thick.

20 Take the gingerbread cutters and stamp out shapes from your dough. Dip the cutter in flour every time you've stamped out a shape (**J**).

21 Gently lift the shapes out of the sheet of dough and arrange them on the prepared baking sheet (**K**).

22 Now allow the shapes to rest and rise in your kitchen for a minimum of 2–4 hours, if it's a fairly warm place. If it's not very warm, you can leave them to rest and rise for 8–24 hours on your work surface, but if you do this, cover them with a sheet of clingfilm/plastic wrap. They will not rise very much because it's hard for the air bubbles to push through the sugar and butter in the dough!

23 When you are ready to bake the gingerbread family, preheat the oven to 220°C (425°F) Gas 7 and put a deep roasting tray in the bottom of the oven.

24 Just before baking, poke holes with a wooden skewer or a chopstick in the dough people to make eyes, buttons and whatever else you like! (**L**)

25 **Ask an adult to help you** put the baking tray in the preheated oven and pour a cup of water into the hot roasting tray in the bottom of the oven: this will form steam and help the gingerbread to form a lovely crust.

26 Lower the oven temperature to 180°C (350°F) Gas 4.

27 Bake the gingerbread for 15–20 minutes until they are starting to go brown around the edges. **Check them after 10 minutes to see how they're doing, but ask an adult to help with this.** If one side of the gingerbread people are getting slightly darker than the other, turn the tray around 180°.

28 Using oven mitts, carefully transfer the gingerbread people to a wire rack to cool before enjoying with your friends!

A

B

Ingredients: Tiger Topping

90 g/¾ cup rice flour

10 g/1 heaping tablespoon cocoa powder

6 g/2½ teaspoons ground ginger

6 g/1½ teaspoons caster/granulated sugar

130 g/130 ml/½ cup water, warm

2 g fresh yeast or 1 g/¼ teaspoon dried/active dry yeast

Ingredients: Dough

300 g/2⅓ cups white strong/bread flour, plus extra for dusting

100 g/⅔ cup crystallized ginger, roughly chopped

7 g/1 tablespoon ground ginger

3 g/¾ teaspoon salt

40 g/2½ tablespoons butter, melted

150 g/⅔ cup whole milk, warmed

12 g fresh or 6 g/1½ teaspoons dried/active dry yeast

30 g/2 tablespoons runny honey

1 egg

Equipment:

4 large mixing bowls

measuring jug/pitcher

small mixing bowl

wooden spoon or Danish whisk

small saucepan

plastic scraper

baking tray lined with parchment paper

deep roasting tray

Makes 1 loaf

Ginger Bread with Tiger (or Giraffe) Topping

This amazing-looking bread is so-called because it looks a lot like the pattern on a tiger's (or giraffe's) back, don't you think? The distinctive dark colour is down to the fact it contains everyone's favourite ingredient – cocoa powder!

1 First, we're going to make the tiger topping. Weigh out the flour, cocoa powder, ground ginger and sugar, add to a large mixing bowl and mix thoroughly with a wooden spoon or Danish whisk.

2 Add the warm water to a small mixing bowl. Weigh out the yeast and add it to the water (**A**) (depending on which type of yeast you're using – **see page 22**, unless you're using instant/quick dry yeast or fast-acting yeast, in which case **see page 17**.

3 Once the yeast is ready to go (dissolved or activated), pour it into the large bowl containing the flour and cocoa powder mixture.

4 Mix to a smooth paste with a Danish whisk or a wooden spoon and leave to one side covered with an upturned small mixing bowl or a shower cap. Leave it in a warm place to start bubbling away!

5 To make the gingerbread dough, in the second large mixing bowl, mix the strong/bread flour, chopped crystallized ginger, ground ginger and salt together thoroughly and set aside. **This is the dry mixture.**

6 Warm the milk up over a low heat in a small saucepan and then add it to the third large mixing bowl.

7 Weigh out the yeast and then dissolve or activate it in the warm milk depending on which type of yeast you're using. **This is the wet mixture (B).**

8 In the fourth large mixing bowl, add the melted butter and set aside.

9 Add the **honey, egg and the dry mixture to the wet mixture**. Mix until it forms a rough dough (**C**).

10 Tip the dough into the large bowl containing the melted butter (**D**). Cover with an upturned small mixing bowl or a shower cap. Let the dough rest for 10 minutes.

11 Squash the dough into a pancake shape to flatten out any lumps (**E**).

12 Lift a portion of the dough up from the side and fold it into the middle (**F**). Then turn the bowl 90° clockwise and lift another portion of the dough up from the side and into the middle. Repeat this process until you've lifted and folded the dough 10 times. Now turn the dough over.

13 Wet your finger and make a fairly deep mark in the middle of the dough to show that you've kneaded the dough once (**G**). Cover the bowl with the smaller bowl that originally contained the flour or a shower cap and leave the dough to rest on your work surface for 10 minutes.

14 Repeat steps 12 and 13 **three more times** (**H**) so you will have kneaded the dough a total of 4 times. You should now have 4 finger marks in the dough (**I**).

15 Cover the dough and leave it to rest for 1 hour. The dough should be smooth and elastic. If not, knead the dough another 1–2 times.

16 After 1 hour, remove the upturned bowl (**J**). Gently punch down on the dough to release the trapped air.

17 Sprinkle a little white strong/bread flour onto a work surface. Remove the dough from the bowl using a plastic scraper and place on the work surface (**K**).

18 Shape the dough into a ball (**see steps 11–14 on page 42**) (**L**) (**M**).

19 Remove the upturned bowl or shower cap covering the tiger topping (**N**).

20 Use the pastry brush to paint the mixture generously onto the dough (**O**).

21 Leave the dough to rise for 1 hour. If your kitchen is fairly draughty, you'll need to cover the dough with a clean large upturned mixing bowl, because otherwise a thick skin will form. If your kitchen isn't draughty, you won't need to cover the dough. If you're not sure about how draughty your kitchen is, just cover it to be on the safe side!

22 While the dough is rising, preheat your oven to 220°C (425°F) Gas 7 and place a deep roasting tray on the bottom surface of the oven.

23 After 1 hour, cracks and patterns will appear on the surface of the dough (**P**).

24 Gently paint on another coating of tiger topping with the pastry brush.

P

25 Place the loaf in the preheated oven and pour a cup of water into the roasting tray in the oven (**ask an adult to help with this**), then lower the oven temperature to 180°C (350°F) Gas 4.

26 Bake for 20–30 minutes until golden brown. Check that it's baked by tapping it on the bottom. If it sounds hollow, it's ready! Let the loaf cool on a wire rack before you slice it (**ask an adult to help with this**).

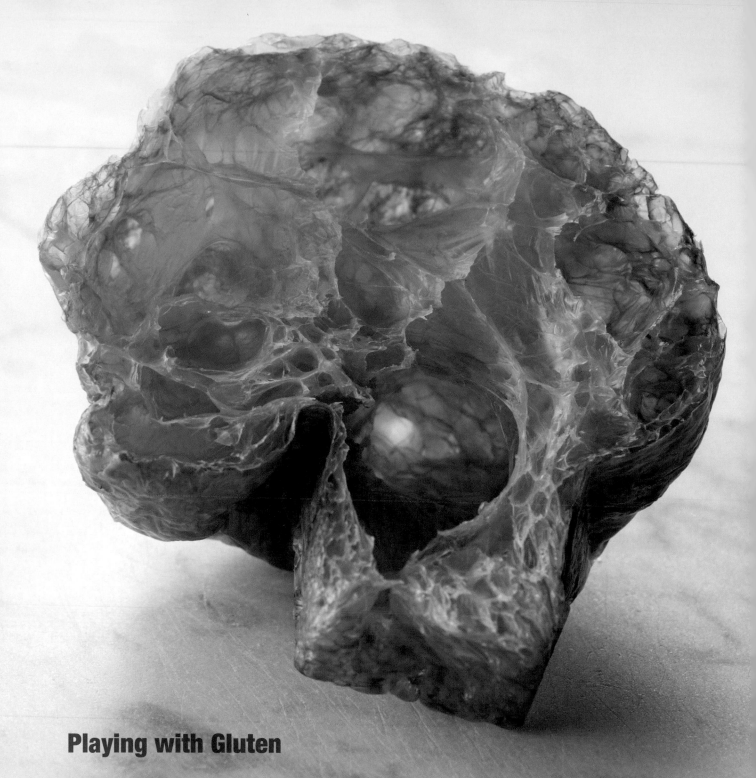

Playing with Gluten

Flour contains two types of protein, which form gluten when they're combined with water. Gluten is a strong, sticky, rubbery substance, which can absorb about twice its weight in water. It is made up of a continuous network of fine strands. It is this network that forms the structure of bread dough and the texture of bread. This experiment explores some of gluten's amazing properties.

Ingredients:

1 x quantity raw dough from the Basic Bread recipe (page 22)

Equipment:

large bowl

colander or sieve

deep roasting tray

pastry brush, for greasing the pan

100-g/3½-oz. capacity miniature loaf pan or ramekin, greased with vegetable oil

1 Put the raw dough in the large bowl (**A**). Pour in enough cold water to come ¾ of the way up the bowl.

2 Now start "washing" the dough in the water: to do this, put your hands in the bowl and squeeze and squash the dough between your fingers.

3 Keep doing this until the water turns nice and milky and the lump of dough feels stringy and stretchy (**B**). You shouldn't be able to see any more white, doughy bits. This might take a few minutes.

4 Now take the stringy dough out of the bowl and put it in the colander or sieve in the sink (**C**). Pour cold water over the dough in the colander and keep squeezing it with your hands to get rid of even more white, milky liquid. Pick the dough up and stretch it – it will fall apart very easily. Now leave it for 15–30 minutes while you go and do something else!

5 After 15–30 minutes, the dough in the colander will have drained, relaxed and become very elastic. This is the gluten from the flour that you originally used to make the dough. Pick it up and have a go at stretching it. See how strong it is and how thinly you can stretch it. Can you believe how much the texture and feel of it has changed?! Fold it over and over onto itself a few times, then shape it roughly into a ball.

6 **Ask an adult to help you** preheat the oven to 250℃, (480°F) Gas 9. Put the roasting tray in the bottom of the oven.

7 Dab the pastry brush in vegetable oil and wipe the brush all over the inside of the loaf pan to grease it. Put the blob of gluten inside the pan (**D**).

8 Once the oven is at the right temperature, **ask an adult to help you** put the loaf pan on the middle shelf. Make sure there's quite a bit of space above it because the gluten will rise a lot!

9 Fill a cup with water, then carefully – without burning yourself on the oven shelf – pour the water into the roasting tray in the bottom of the oven. Lower the oven temperature to 200℃ (400°F) Gas 6.

10 After about 10–15 minutes, look through the oven door and you will notice that the little loaf has expanded quite dramatically. This is normal! The gluten is so stretchy that bubbles inside it are filling with steam in the hot oven and stretching the gluten! Imagine that this is what's happening on a small scale inside every loaf of bread you make, helping to make the dough stretchy and the baked bread light and nicely chewy.

11 After 35 minutes, lower the oven temperature to 180℃ (350°F) Gas 4 and bake for a further 15 minutes. This will toast the exterior to make it crispier.

12 When it has finished baking, **ask an adult to help you** take the loaf pan out of the oven and carefully tip the loaf onto a wire rack to cool (**E**).

13 When it has completely cooled down, **ask an adult to help you** slice it.

Note how the air has been trapped in the loaf and how rubbery its texture is. Have a taste – what do you think? You can actually buy this wheat protein in shops – it's called "seitan". It is very good for vegetarians or vegans who need to eat protein and cannot get it from meat or animal products.

Ingredients:

1 x quantity raw dough from the Basic Bread recipe (see page 22)

black and white sesame seeds

sea salt

Equipment:

large bowl

colander

pastry brush

baking sheet lined with parchment paper

palette knife

Playing with Starch

Starch provides "food" for yeast to feed on. It also interacts with gluten during baking. The gluten breaks down and releases water, which is taken up by the starch, making the gluten rigid. This is the reason why loaves of bread don't collapse. Starch can also be quite tasty, as you'll find out here!

1 Follow **steps 1–4** on **page 131**.

2 After 30–60 minutes, you will notice that the milky water has separated into two liquids (**A**).

3 Stick your finger gently in the bowl and touch the bottom-most white layer – it should feel a little crunchy and squeaky.

4 Take a spoon and carefully scoop the top liquid out of the bowl and down the sink. You want to leave the bottom-most, thick white layer in the bowl. This is the starch from the wheat flour and this is what yeast converts to sugar (**see pages 16–19**), which in turn creates bubbles and causes the bread to rise.

5 Ask an adult to help you preheat the oven to 200°C (400°F) Gas 6.

6 Take the pastry brush and brush the thick, white liquid over the parchment paper on the baking sheet (**B**). It will be difficult at first as the mixture might separate but keep going until you have a complete puddle of the liquid.

7 Sprinkle a few black and white sesame seeds and a little sea salt all over the puddle (**C**).

8 Once the oven has reached the right temperature, **ask an adult to help you** put the baking sheet on the middle shelf and bake for 5–10 minutes until it looks golden. It will look like a large sheet of crisp wafer.

9 When it has finished baking, take the parchment paper out of the oven, and use a palette knife to tip the wafer onto a wire rack to cool. When it's cool, snap a piece off and enjoy!

sweet treats

Frosted Carrot Bread

Ingredients:

200 g/1½ cups white strong/bread flour, plus extra for dusting

2 g/½ teaspoon salt

100 g/¾ cup carrot, coarsely grated

20 g/2 tablespoons crystallized/candied ginger, cut into small pieces

2 g/1 teaspoon ground cinnamon

150 g/150 ml/⅔ cup water, warm

4 g fresh or 2 g/½ teaspoon dried/active dry yeast

20 g/2 tablespoons dark brown sugar

10 g/2 teaspoons sunflower oil

Ingredients for the Frosting:

300 g/10 oz. cream cheese

100 g/¾ cup icing/confectioners' sugar, plus extra for dusting

ground cinnamon, for dusting

Equipment:

3 small mixing bowls

measuring jug/pitcher

2 large mixing bowls

Danish whisk (optional)

wooden spoon

shower cap (optional)

plastic scraper

18-cm/7-in. round sandwich pan greased with vegetable oil and sprinkled with flour

pastry brush

balloon whisk

Serves 8–10

A spin-off of the ever-popular carrot cake, this variant is made with crystallized/candied ginger, really bringing out the sweetness in the carrot. With the delicious frosting, this really is a treat, but it tastes great without it, too!

1 In one of the small mixing bowls, mix the strong/bread flour and salt together thoroughly and set aside. **This is the dry mixture.**

2 In another small mixing bowl, mix the grated carrot, chopped crystallized ginger and the ground cinnamon together and set aside.

3 Weigh out the water in the measuring jug/pitcher and transfer ¾ of it into a large mixing bowl.

4 Weigh out the yeast and add the yeast to the water (depending on which type of yeast you're using – **see page 22**, unless you're using instant/quick dry yeast or fast-acting yeast, in which case **see page 17**. **This is the wet mixture** (**A**, over the page).

5 Add the brown sugar to the wet mixture and stir with a Danish whisk or a wooden spoon until the sugar has dissolved (**B**, over the page).

6 Add the dry mixture and the carrot mixture to the wet mixture (**C**, over the page).

7 Mix with a Danish whisk or a wooden spoon until it forms a rough dough. If the dough is quite stiff, add a little of the remaining water (**D**, over the page).

8 Coat the bottom of another large mixing bowl with the sunflower oil. Place the dough into the oil, then cover the dough with a shower cap or the small mixing bowl that contained the dry mixture (**E**, over the page).

9 Let the dough rest for 10 minutes (**F**, over the page). The dough should be a bit sticky.

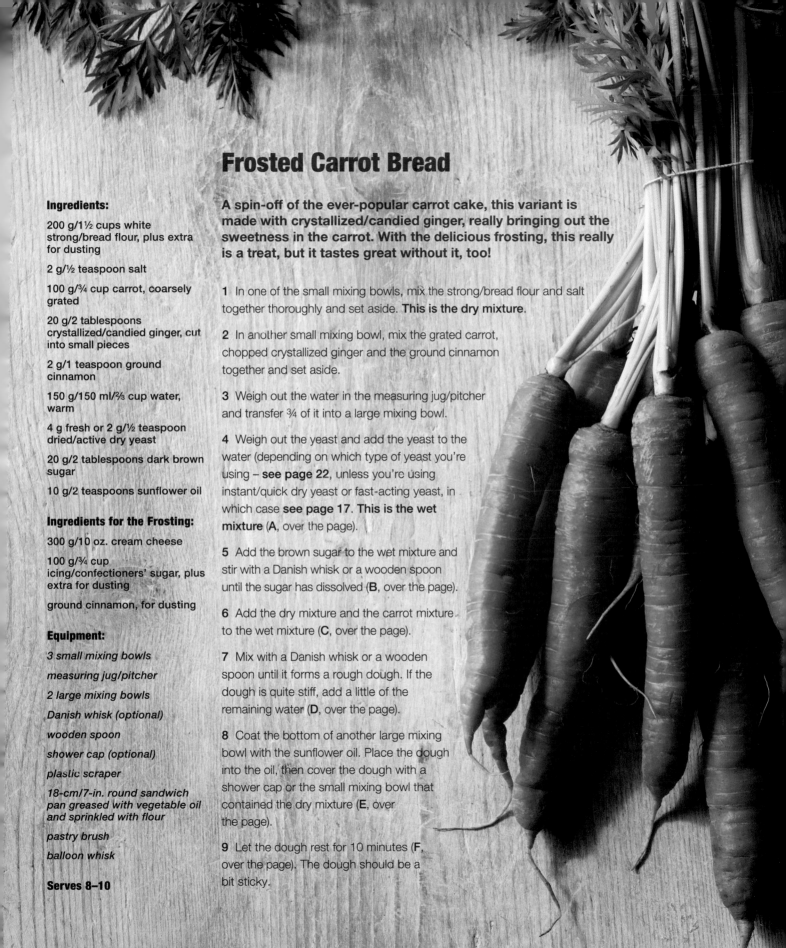

10 **Lift** a portion of the dough up from one side and **fold** it into the middle. Turn the bowl 90° clockwise.

11 Repeat step 10 **nine** times until you've **lifted and folded the dough a total of 10 times**. You've now kneaded the dough once.

12 Now turn the dough over. Wet your finger and make a fairly deep mark in the middle of the dough to show that you've kneaded it once.

13 Cover the dough with the small bowl again or the shower cap and leave it to rest for 10 minutes.

14 Repeat steps 10–13 three more times, so you will have kneaded the dough a total of **4 times.**

15 Cover the dough with the small bowl again or the shower cap and leave it to rise for 1 hour.

16 After 1 hour, gently punch down the dough to release the trapped air.

17 Lightly flour a work surface and transfer the dough to it from the bowl using a plastic scraper.

18 Shape the dough into a ball by taking a corner of it and folding it over to the opposite side, then turn the dough 90° clockwise. Repeat another 4–5 times and then turn the dough over. Tuck in the underneath of the dough with your fingers as you rotate the dough clockwise until you've formed a tight, rounded ball.

19 Place the dough into the prepared sandwich pan and cover with a clean shower cap (**G**). Place in a warm place to rise for 20–35 minutes. If your kitchen isn't that warm, follow the instructions on **page 28** and check it every 15 minutes.

20 When the dough has risen so that it's level with the top of the pan, you can remove the shower cap or bowl (**H**) and remove the pan from the oven, if you left in there.

21 Set the oven temperature to 220°C (425°F) Gas 7.

22 Place the sandwich pan in the oven (once it's heated up), then lower the temperature to 180°C (350°F) Gas 4.

23 Bake for around 20 minutes until golden brown. If you want to check whether it's properly baked, **ask an adult to help you** lift the pan out of the pan with oven mitts and tap the bottom with your knuckles. If it sounds hollow, it's ready. Leave to cool on a wire rack.

24 While the bread is cooling, make the cream cheese frosting. In another small mixing bowl mix the cream cheese and half the icing/confectioners' sugar with a balloon whisk until it is nice and smooth. Once it's smooth, taste it to see if it is sweet enough. If not, add more icing/confectioners' sugar.

25 Once the Carrot Bread is cool, **ask an adult to help you** cut it horizontally into 2 pieces with a serrated knife.

26 Spread half of the cream cheese frosting on the bottom half of the Carrot Bread with a knife (**I**) and place the top half of the Carrot Bread back on top. Spread the rest of the frosting on the top of the top half and sprinkle the ground cinnamon and a little icing/confectioners' sugar to finish. Now cut and serve!

Sticky Raspberry Buns

Ingredients:

200 g/1⅔ cups white strong/bread flour, plus extra for dusting

5 g/2 teaspoons baking powder, sifted if lumpy

50 g/¼ cup caster/granulated sugar, plus extra for coating the buns

2 g/½ teaspoon salt

50 g/3 tablespoons whole milk

1 egg, lightly beaten

2 g/½ teaspoon pure vanilla extract

50 g/3 tablespoons butter (cold), chopped into cubes

raspberry jam/jelly

Makes about 8

Equipment:

large mixing bowl

wooden spoon

small mixing bowl

plastic scraper

8 large muffin cups

large muffin tray (with room for 6–8 muffins) or baking tray lined with parchment paper

Based on an old-fashioned traditional English recipe and much like a classic jam tart, these buns are a perfect sweet treat. It's hard to resist dunking your finger in the jammy centre, but be patient and wait until they've cooled first!

1 In the large mixing bowl mix the flour, baking powder, sugar and salt together thoroughly with your hands or a wooden spoon. **This is the dry mixture**.

2 In the small mixing bowl, mix the milk, egg and vanilla extract together with a wooden spoon and set aside. **This is the wet mixture.**

3 Add the cold cubed butter to the dry mixture with your hands (**A**).

4 Rub the dry mixture and butter with your fingertips until it feels crumbly (**B**) (**C**).

5 Add the wet mixture to the dry mixture (**D**) and mix together until evenly combined. Be careful not to mix for too long, though, as otherwise the mixture will taste chewy once it's baked, so just mix it until all the flour is incorporated.

B

C

D

E

F

G

H

6 Lightly flour a work surface. Transfer the mixture to the work surface with a plastic scraper and sprinkle the top lightly with flour (**E**).

7 Use the plastic scaper to divide the mixture into little portions (around 50 g/1¾ oz.) and roll them into balls (**F**).

8 Preheat your oven to 200°C (390°F) Gas 6.

9 Fill a small bowl with sugar and roll the balls in the bowl (**G**).

10 Place the sugar-coated balls into the muffin cups or place on the prepared baking tray and flatten the buns a little. If the sugar does not stick to the buns, dip them in water then coat with sugar.

11 Make an indentation in each bun using your finger (**H**) and fill them with jam, using a spoon (**I**).

12 Bake in the preheated oven for 20 minutes until light golden brown; turn the tray after 10 minutes (**ask an adult to help with this**). Leave the buns to cool on a wire rack and serve.

"My favourite thing was using my hands to mix the ingredients, squeezing it through my fingers and putting the jam in the holes. And licking my fingers afterwards!"

Charlotte (Aged 6)

Banana Bread

Ingredients:

120 g/1 cup white strong/bread flour, plus extra for dusting

80 g/⅔ cup wholemeal/ whole-wheat flour

2 g/½ teaspoon salt

1 banana (very ripe)

60 g/¼ cup runny honey

2 g/1 teaspoon grated lemon zest

1 egg, lightly beaten

10 g/10 ml/2 teaspoons water, warm

20 g/20 ml/4 teaspoons whole milk, warm

12 g fresh or 6 g/1½ teaspoons dried/active dry yeast

20 g/4 teaspoons unsalted butter, melted

Equipment:

small saucepan

3 small mixing bowls

2 large mixing bowls

plastic scraper

shower cap (optional)

pastry brush, for greasing the pan

500-g/6 x 4-in. loaf pan, greased with vegetable oil

deep roasting tray

Makes 1 loaf

Freshly baked banana bread with chocolate spread takes me back to summer afternoons in South Africa as a child. This is slightly different as it's bread (made with yeast) rather than a cake. It's perfect for using up overripe bananas!

1 Melt the butter in a small saucepan over a low heat and set aside in a small mixing bowl (**Ask an adult to help with this**).

2 In another small mixing bowl mix the flours and salt together thoroughly and set aside. **This is the dry mixture**.

3 In a third small mixing bowl, mash the bananas with a fork and mix together with the honey and the lemon zest (**A**). Mix the egg into the banana mixture and set aside. **This is the banana mixture**.

4 Add the water and milk to a large mixing bowl.

5 Weigh out the yeast and add the yeast to the water and milk mixture. **This is the wet mixture**. If you're using dried/active dry yeast, soak it for around 10 minutes or until it floats to the top and starts to bubble slightly. If you're using fresh yeast, dissolve it in warm water with your hands. If you're using instant/quick dry yeast or fast-acting yeast, see page 17.

6 Add the dry mixture, and the banana and egg mixture to the wet mixture and mix until it forms a **rough dough** (**B**).

7 Add the melted butter to a separate large mixing bowl and then transfer the dough into the bowl using a plastic scraper (**C**).

8 Cover the dough with a shower cap or with the small bowl that contained the dry mixture and leave to stand for 10 minutes.

9 Squash the dough into a pancake shape with your fingers to flatten out any lumps.

10 Lift a portion of the dough up from the side and fold it into the middle. Turn the bowl 90° clockwise.

11 **Repeat step 10** nine times until you've lifted and folded the dough **10** times. Now turn the dough over.

12 Wet your finger and make a fairly deep mark in the middle of the dough to show that you've kneaded it once. Cover the bowl with a shower cap or with the small bowl that contained the dry mixture and leave the dough to rest on your work surface for 10 minutes.

13 Repeat steps 10–12 **three more times** so that you have kneaded the dough **4 times in total**. Make sure to cover the mixture between kneads for 10 minutes and remember to mark the dough to remind you of the number of times you've kneaded it. Don't worry if the dough feels soft, it will be. The final time, cover the dough and leave it to rise for **1 hour.**

14 After 1 hour, the dough will have grown in volume (**D**). Gently punch down on it to release the trapped air.

E

F

G

15 Lightly flour a work surface and shape the banana bread into a loaf (**see page 26 for instructions on how to shape a loaf**).

16 Place the dough into the prepared loaf pan seam-side down and cover with a shower cap or a clean large mixing bowl (**F**). If your kitchen is fairly warm, you can just leave the loaf pan to rise for about 20–30 minutes.

If your kitchen isn't that warm, **follow the instructions on page 28**.

17 Once the dough has risen so that the top of the loaf is about 2 cm/¾ in. above the surface of the pan, it's ready to bake. Remove the loaf pan from the oven, if you left it to rise in there.

18 Preheat your oven to 200°C (400°F) Gas 6 and place the roasting tray on the bottom surface.

19 Place the loaf pan in the preheated oven and pour a cup of water into the hot tray to form steam (**ask an adult to help with this**). Lower the oven temperature to 180°C (350°F) Gas 4.

20 Bake for 20–30 minutes until golden brown. Allow to cool on a wire rack before slicing it and spreading it with a nice thick layer of chocolate spread!

Simple Chocolate and Cherry Stollen

My baking career began in a German-style bakery in South Africa, and so stollen – the traditional German Christmas-time specialty – is quite dear to me. I've added the flavours of the Black Forest – chocolate and cherry – to make it extra special!

A

Ingredients:

12 g/1 tablespoon caster/granulated sugar

16 g/1 tablespoon water, boiling

60 g/2 oz. dark chocolate (70% cocoa solids), melted

200 g/2½ tablespoons Morello cherries

20 g/2½ tablespoons white strong/bread flour

12 g fresh or 6 g/1½ teaspoons dried/active dry yeast

20 g/20 ml/4 teaspoons water, warm

240 g/2 cups white strong/bread flour, plus extra for dusting

100 g/3.5 oz. dark chocolate (70% cocoa solids) chips or good dark chocolate cut into small pieces

80 g/5 tablespoons butter, (unsalted or salted) softened

60 g/⅓ cup caster/granulated sugar

2 g or ½ teaspoon salt

½ teaspoon pure vanilla extract

2 eggs, lightly beaten

icing/confectioners' sugar, for dusting

Equipment:

tray or plate lined with parchment paper

colander

3 large mixing bowls

shower cap (optional)

rolling pin

baking tray lined with parchment paper

3 small mixing bowls

deep roasting tray

colander

Makes 12–14 slices, depending on thickness

1 **First make the chocolate log**. In a small mixing bowl melt the 12 g/1 tablespoon sugar in the boiling water (**ask an adult to help you**) and stir the mixture until all the sugar has dissolved.

2 Mix in the melted chocolate until it is a smooth glossy mixture.

3 Place the mixture on the prepared tray or plate and allow it to cool in the refrigerator. As it cools, you'll be able to shape into an 18 cm/7 in. log (**A**) and keep in the refrigerator until ready to use.

4 Drain the morello cherries, then place them in another small mixing bowl and set aside.

5 Put the 20 g/2½ tablespoons white strong/bread flour in a large mixing bowl and set aside.

6 In another large mixing bowl, weigh out the yeast, add it to the warm water and stir it until it has dissolved (unless using instant/quick dry yeast or fast-acting yeast, in which case, see page 17). **This is the yeast mixture**.

7 Add the set-aside flour to the yeast and mix it into a paste. Leave the mixture to rise and cover it with a shower cap or an upturned bowl until it has doubled in volume, about 15–30 minutes.

8 In another small mixing bowl put the 240 g/2 cups white strong/bread flour and the dark chocolate chips (or pieces) and set aside. **This is the flour and chocolate mixture.**

9 In the third large mixing bowl beat the butter, the 60 g/⅓ cup sugar, salt and the pure vanilla extract until soft (**B**).

10 Add the lightly beaten eggs into the butter mixture, a little at a time. Once all the egg is incorporated, stop beating. If the mixture separates and goes all lumpy, slowly mix in some of the flour and chocolate mixture to bind it together (**C**).

11 Add the **flour and chocolate mixture** to **the yeast mixture** then add the **butter mixture** (**D**). **Make sure you add the flour mixture to the yeast mixture before adding the butter mixture.**

12 Mix until it all comes together and it looks like a rough dough (**E**).

C

E

F

G

13 Cover with the small mixing bowl (**F**) or a shower cap and leave it to stand for 10 minutes to rise.

14 Lift a portion of the dough up from the side and fold it into the middle. Turn the bowl 90° clockwise.

15 Repeat step 14 until you've lifted and folded the dough 10 times or until the dough resists. Leave to stand for 10 minutes.

16 Repeat steps 14 and 15 another 3 times, remembering to cover the bowl between kneading.

17 Allow the dough to rise (proof) for 1 hour, covered with the upturned bowl or shower cap again.

18 Once the dough has proofed for an hour and has increased in volume (**G**), gently punch down the dough to release the trapped air.

19 Lightly sprinkle a work surface with flour. Transfer the dough to the floured work surface, and use a rolling pin to roll the dough (**H**) into a rectangle about 1 cm/⅜ in. thick and around 25 cm/10 in. wide.

20 Press the whole Morello cherries into the dough. Remove the chocolate log from the refrigerator and place it one-third of the way up the dough (**I**).

21 Fold the sides of the dough over the chocolate log, pressing it down lightly (**J**), then begin rolling it up (**K**).

I

J   K

L M N O

22 Place the loaf seam side down on the prepared baking tray (**L**).

23 Gently press down the right side of the dough to widen it. Do the same with the left side of the dough (**M**).

24 Cover the dough with the large mixing bowl. If your kitchen is fairly warm, you can leave it on the work surface to rise for around 30 minutes until it has nearly doubled in volume (**N**). **If your kitchen isn't that warm, follow the instructions on page 28**, but make sure you turn the oven off at the right time, because otherwise the chocolate will melt!

25 Preheat the oven to 200°C (400°F) Gas 6 and place a deep roasting tray at the base.

26 Before baking, place the stollen on the baking tray in the refrigerator for about **30 minutes**. This will harden the

chocolate, especially the centre, so it does not melt while baking and leak out.

27 Place the stollen in the preheated oven and pour a cup of water into the hot tray to form steam (**ask an adult to help with this**).

28 Lower the oven temperature to 180°C (350°F) Gas 4.

29 Bake for around 20 minutes until golden brown (**O**).

30 Carefully remove the baking tray using oven mitts (**ask an adult to help**). Using one oven mitt to hold the stollen, check that it's baked by tapping it on the bottom with the knuckles of your other hand. If you hear a hollow sound, it's ready.

31 Allow to cool on a wire rack. Once it has cooled, dust it generously with icing/confectioners' sugar and cut into lovely thick slices!

 Fascinating Fact:

A traditional festive treat in Germany, stollen dates back to before 1400. It was originally made with flour, yeast, oil and water as the use of butter was banned during the season of Advent. The ban was only lifted by the Pope 90 years later!

Bread and Butter Pudding

This recipe is so easy to make and with delicious results. It tastes even better with slightly older bread, so remember not to throw it away! You can also make French toast/eggy bread from the mixture to give yourself a treat for a weekday breakfast.

Ingredients:

500 g/500 ml/2 cups whole milk

100 g/½ cup caster/granulated sugar

1 teaspoon pure vanilla extract

3 eggs

7–10 slices of white bread, cut about 5 mm/⅕ in. thick

150 g/1¼ cups raisins

butter, softened (unsalted or salted)

50 g/¼ cup caster/granulated sugar mixed with 1 tablespoon ground cinnamon

Equipment:

small mixing bowl

balloon whisk

26 x 18-cm/10 x 7-in. or 30 x 20-cm/ 12 x 8-in. oval-shaped Pyrex baking dish, greased with butter

Serves 4

1 First make the custard milk mixture: add the milk to a small mixing bowl, then dissolve the sugar and the pure vanilla extract in it using a balloon whisk.

2 Once the sugar is dissolved add the eggs and mix with the balloon whisk until you have a smooth mixture. Put the mixture to one side.

3 See how many slices of bread will fit in a criss-cross pattern into your Pyrex dish, then spread each slice generously with butter.

4 Grease the Pyrex dish with butter and sprinkle ¾ of the raisins on the bottom. Place the buttered bread back in the dish, then sprinkle the remaining raisins on top.

5 Whisk the custard mixture that you put to one side and pour it on top of the bread. The bread will float up to the top of the dish, but don't worry, this is perfectly normal!

6 Allow to soak for 1 hour in the fridge so the custard mixture will be absorbed into the bread.

7 Preheat the oven to 100°C (210°F) and, once the oven has heated up, bake for **50–70 minutes** until the custard has set. **The reason that we bake it at this low temperature is so the custard doesn't separate and go all lumpy**.

8 You can check to see if it's ready by carefully removing the pan from the oven using oven mitts and shaking the pan from side to side (**ask an adult to help with this**). If the custard is set but wobbles slightly when you shake it, it's ready!

9 Sprinkle the top with the sugar and cinnamon mix and allow to cool before serving.

Suppliers and stockists

UK

Fresh yeast can be bought from bakeries and most supermarkets with in-store bakeries.

Shipton Mill
Long Newnton
Tetbury
Gloucestershire GL8 8RP
Te: +44 (0)1666 505050
www.shipton-mill.com
For many, many types of organic flour, milled on site, available to buy online in small or large quantities. They also stock fresh yeast, organic yeast and proofing/dough-rising baskets. Their website is also a good reference for the mechanics of flour and grains.

Doves Farm
Doves Farm Foods Ltd
Salisbury Road
Hungerford
Berkshire RG17 0RF
Tel: +44 (0)1488 684880
www.dovesfarm.co.uk
Like Shipton Mill, Doves Farm supplies many, many types of organic flour, milled on site and available to buy online in small or large quantities, as well as all sorts of other organic products. They stock a large range of proofing/dough-rising baskets in all sizes and shapes

www.brotformen.de
Tel: +49 (0)34 364 522 87
German supplier of proofing/dough-rising baskets in all manner of shapes and sizes.

Bakery Bits
1 Orchard Units, Duchy Road
Honiton
Devon EX14 1YD
Tel: +44 (0)1404 565656
www.bakerybits.co.uk
Online supplier of every kind of tool, utensil and equipment needed to bake bread.

Lakeland
Tel: +44 (0)1539 488100
www.lakeland.co.uk
Stockists of bakeware and cookware, with branches around the UK, as well as an excellent website.

Divertimenti
Tel: +44 (0)870 129 5026
www.divertimenti.co.uk
Cookware stockist, with branches in London and Cambridge, as well as an online store.

Nisbets
Tel: +44 (0)845 140 5555
www.nisbets.co.uk
Enormous range of catering equipment to buy online, including loaf pans and more, plus branches in London and Bristol.

The Traditional Cornmillers Guild
www.tcmg.org.uk
For details of individual mills around the UK.

US

King Arthur Flour
Tel: +1 800 827 6836
www.kingarthurflour.com
America's oldest – and one of the best – flour company. Flours are unbleached and never bromated. Their great selection of flours includes 9-grain flour blend, malted wheat flakes, Irish-style wholemeal/whole-wheat flour, French-style flour for baguettes, European-style artisan bread flour, as well as sugar, yeast in bulk, sourdough starters, baking pans, proofing/dough-rising baskets, bread/pizza peels and other bakeware and equipment.

Bob's Red Mill
Tel: +1 (503) 654 3215
www.bobsredmill.com
Online supplier of traditional and gluten-free flours, plus grains and seeds.

Hodgson Mill
Tel: +1 800 347 0105
www.hodgsonmill.com
Suppliers of all-natural, whole grains and stoneground products.

Breadtopia
Tel: +1 800 469 7989
www.breadtopia.com
From dough scrapers to rising baskets, and sourdough starters, this Iowa-based company has every gadget and pan an artisan bread baker could ever want.

La Cuisine – The Cook's Resource
Tel: +1 800 521 1176
www.lacuisineus.com
Fine bakeware including oval and round proofing/dough-rising baskets, loaf pans in every size and bread/pizza peels.

Crate & Barrel
Tel: +1 630 369 4464
www.crateandbarrel.com
Good stockist of bakeware online and in stores throughout the country.

Sur la table
Tel: +1 800 243 0852
www.surlatable.com
Good stockist of bakeware online and in stores throughout the country.

Williams-Sonoma
Tel: +1 877 812 6235
www.williams-sonoma.com
Good stockist of bakeware online and in stores throughout the country.

Index

acknowledgments

I would like to thank the following people for their help with this book:

Steve Painter with his great talent in taking pictures that tells the story of Making Bread Together, his patience and attention to detail.

To the children: Noah my son; my nieces Alissa and Lilia; Ayse, Charlotte, Kitty, Marley, Mimi, Nico, Nilu"fer and Sami for taking part in the book. Also to Amanda and Fergus and Shelly for allowing us to use their kitchens to take photographs.

Thanks to John Lister from Shipton Mill and Jethro Marriage from Doves Farm for sponsoring the flour used in the book. To Sonja for the great organic yeast from Agrano.

Thanks to The School Of Artisan Food where I teach for lending me some of the small equipment used in the book as props. Also to David Carter for his words of wisdom and helping with some of the research and text for the book. Thanks to Dave Redding for making the wooden peels and to Andy Forbes for showing us exactly how wheat is harvested!

I would also like to thank Celine Hughes (with the beginning stages) and Nathan Joyce for their patience and understanding in editing the book and Lucy McKelvie for food styling on pages 65, 81, 100, 101 and 154.

My wife, Lisa, my biggest supporter, for her enthusiasm and patience through the whole project.

Lastly, to everyone that had a little say in the book, tasting the breads or testing the recipes, a big thank you to all of you.